BRITAIN'S

FR

3

WILDGuides

PRINCETON
press.princeton.edu

Published by Princeton University Press,
41 William Street, Princeton, New Jersey 08540
In the United Kingdom: Princeton University Press, 6 Oxford Street,
Woodstock, Oxfordshire OX20 1TW
nathist.press.princeton.edu

British Library Cataloging-in-Publication Data is available

Library of Congress Control Number 2012956135
ISBN 978-0-691-15678-1

Production and design by **WILD**Guides Ltd., Old Basing, Hampshire UK.
Printed in Singapore

10 9 8 7 6 5 4 3 2 1

Contents

Introduction

Fish comprise a diverse group of some 32,000 species of limbless vertebrates and are found in aquatic habitats around the world, ranging from upland lakes and rivers to deep oceans. Most fish, and certainly all of the freshwater fishes of Britain and Ireland, are 'cold-blooded' (technically known as 'ectothermic'), their body temperature varying with the ambient water temperature, which has a significant influence on their seasonal behaviour. The term 'fish' is in fact used somewhat loosely, as some are actually not 'true' fishes at all: the lampreys, for example, that occur in the fresh waters of the British Isles, lack jaws, paired fins and have only cartilaginous skeletons. However, all fish swim using fins and breath largely through gills.

Fish play an important part in our lives. They are integral to the food webs and ecosystems of the world's waters, but also have importance as a source of food, cultural identity and recreational opportunity, as well as having spiritual significance. We bring them close to us in garden ponds and in tanks in living rooms and dentists' waiting rooms, a tangible form of connection with the natural world. Yet the fishes of the fresh waters of the British Isles are relatively little known, because the eye for many people stops at the surface film. The freshwater fishes of Britain and Ireland include those resident in rivers, streams, lakes, canals and pools of all sizes, but also those that penetrate seasonally upstream from the brackish waters of estuaries.

Accurate identification of fishes is important in order to determine the health of our waterways, and to understand the recreational, educational and other opportunities they offer. This guide aims to provide the information needed to identify all the fishes that are known to occur in the fresh waters of Britain and Ireland. It contains a comprehensive description of each of the species, yet is presented in easily understood language and graphic content. Its purpose is to help the non-specialist identify the fishes that they find in streams, rivers, pools, lakes and estuaries in Britain and Ireland.

The Dace is a common and widespread fish of flowing fresh waters throughout Britain.

About this book

The emphasis in this book is on simple field identification from basic features (what is known by naturalists as the 'jizz' or 'gestalt'), rather than expecting the reader to develop taxonomic expertise. All 41 species of freshwater fishes that are native to Britain and Ireland are covered, together with 12 that have been introduced. The bulk of the guide comprises individual profiles for these species, highlighting the key identification features and providing notes on their ecology and conservation. Each species is illustrated with a photograph to aid identification.

It is important to note that this book focusses on the identification of adult fishes. Immature fishes can often be very difficult to identify to species, and in many cases their identification is best left to specialists.

To ensure this book is as easy as possible to read, English names are used for the fishes. Scientific (Latin) names are included only in the main species accounts, although they are given for other, non-fish, species where appropriate.

The book provides an introduction to the different aquatic habitats that freshwater fishes inhabit in Britain and Ireland (*page 12*), and information on conservation and legislative issues (*page 132*).

Finding fishes

It is assumed that users of this guide will rely primarily on simple observation. With a stealthy approach, it is quite possible to 'fish watch', particularly in the summer when they are closer to the surface and the water is generally lower and clearer. Spotting fish is significantly aided by polarizing sunglasses to help you see through glare from the water's surface. However, it is important to be aware of the finely tuned senses of the fish you hope to spot. Fish sense vibrations in the water using their lateral line organs, and this includes sensing heavy footfalls – so you must learn to stalk the waterside with care. Also, fish are finely attuned to predators that may attack from above, so make use of the cover of waterside trees and tall bankside vegetation to mask your silhouette, and avoid sharp movements. Stalk the bank top patiently and stealthly, and you may often observe fish behaving naturally and unaware of your presence.

Sunglasses with polarizing lenses help you see fishes through the surface glare, whilst pond nets are helpful for catching smaller fishes in the margins.

If you want to examine a fish closely, a pond net is often helpful – at least for the smaller, shore-hugging species that can be captured this way. Another approach is to ask anglers what species are present, though this will tend to overlook the so-called 'minor species' that are important in aquatic ecosystems.

Other more thorough and quantitative non-destructive survey methods include electrofishing and also seine netting. However, these are expensive, have associated risks, require legal permissions and health and safety training, and are assumed to be beyond the needs of those using this guide.

The conservation value of fishes

Some fish species are of direct nature conservation interest and a few are threatened and afforded legal protection (see *page 132*). For example, all three species of lamprey recorded from Britain and Ireland are listed in both EU and British legislation. Others may proliferate if introduced into new waters to which they are not native, changing the balance of the ecosystems and potentially compromising the conservation of other fish, plant or animal communities.

Smaller fish species and juvenile stages of larger fishes can serve as important links in food chains, feeding on small invertebrates and algae and in turn being fed on by birds such as kingfishers, grebes and terns, as well as predatory fishes. Larger fish such as Pike, Perch and Chub also play key roles in the cycles of food and energy, the life-cycles of parasites, and provide food for other species including birds such as bitterns, herons and cormorants, and mammals such as otters.

Biosecurity

It is important to be very careful to avoid inadvertently spreading organisms between waters when sampling, particularly invasive species. These include, for example, invertebrates such as Signal Crayfish *Pacifastacus leniusculus*, plants such as New Zealand Pigmyweed *Crassula helmsii* and small fish such as Topmouth Gudgeon (see *page 78*). This is achieved by the simple precaution of washing and thoroughly drying, or ideally disinfecting, boots, pond nets or other equipment on or in which small species or their propagules or diseases may be carried.

Signal Crayfish Pacifastacus leniusculus

New Zealand Pigmyweed Crassula helmsii

Introduced species

The fish fauna of fresh waters is probably one of the most manipulated elements of the biodiversity of the British Isles. Common Carp, for example, were repeatedly introduced to these islands from the 15th century onwards. They have since been widely redistributed into still waters for recreational angling purposes. Introduced Common Carp can cause major disruption to ecosystems with which they have not co-evolved, largely due to their habit of stirring up aquatic sediment while feeding, their voracious appetites and rapid growth, and their fecundity: the very attributes that suit them to introduction for aquaculture. Although the Barbel is native to British fresh waters, it too has been associated with ecological changes where it has been introduced, mainly for recreational angling, beyond its natural distribution in eastward-draining rivers from the Thames to those feeding into the Humber.

Alien introductions, both deliberate and accidental, include large and small predators such as the Wels Catfish, Zander and Rainbow Trout, as well as small invasive and problematic species such as Topmouth Gudgeon and Sunbleak. All fish movements, from alien introductions to deliberate translocation of native stock, can also carry with them unwanted parasites and diseases as well as 'stowaway' species.

So, whilst generalizations can be made about the natural distribution of freshwater fishes in our diverse standing and flowing waters, it is important to be prepared for surprises in which nature has had no direct hand.

A number of fish species in the fresh waters of the British Isles are both alien and potentially invasive. The Common Carp, Rainbow Trout, Grass Carp, Orfe, Goldfish, Zander and Wels Catfish have been long-established and are accepted by many people as part of the British fauna, notwithstanding lingering conservation concerns and potential problems inherent in more widespread introductions.

Rainbow Trout is a familiar and widespread introduced species that is native to the Pacific coast of America.

As well as the Rainbow Trout, other American trout species have been introduced to British waters in the past. These include, for example, the Brook Trout *Salvelinus fontinalis* and the Cutthroat Trout *Oncorhynchus clarkii*, which have not become established and are increasingly less available due to concerns about their potential to establish self-sustaining populations. In addition, the Tiger Trout, a hybrid of Brown and Brook Trout, has been introduced into British fisheries in the past, but this practice has ceased today. All species of *Salvelinus* (apart from the native Arctic Charr) are controlled under the *Prohibition of Keeping or Release of Live Fish (Specified Species) Order 1998* (see *page 136*).

However, a number of other, generally smaller, species are more recent introductions, and are giving rise to particular conservation concerns. These species are the Topmouth Gudgeon, Sunbleak, Bitterling, Pumpkinseed Sunfish and Black Bullhead, and they share some or all of the attributes generally considered to predispose aquatic organisms to become invasive:

- Abundant and widely distributed in their original range
- Wide environmental tolerance
- High genetic variability
- Short generation time
- Rapid growth
- Early sexual maturity
- High reproductive capacity
- Broad diet (opportunistic feeding)
- Gregariousness
- Possessing natural mechanisms of rapid dispersal
- Commensal with human activity (e.g. transport in ship ballast water, or trade of ornamental species for aquarists)

It is also worth noting that at least three species of small black American catfish are believed to have been imported into the UK for sale through the aquarist trade: the Black Bullhead, the Brown Bullhead *Ameiurus nebulosus* (formerly *Ictalurus nebulosus*), and the Channel Catfish *Ictalurus punctatus*. All appear to have the capacity to establish viable British populations, the consequences of which are largely unforeseeable but are in all probability seriously negative.

The Orfe is not native to Britain and Ireland but is capable of establishing self-sustaining populations, and has done so locally, threatening the balance of ecosystems.

Life-cycles of British freshwater fishes

All species of British freshwater fish are egg-layers, although this is by no means true for all of the world's fishes. The time of year at which eggs are laid and the spawning strategy vary between fish species and families.

With just one exception, British freshwater fishes of the salmon family seek out clean gravel where they cut depressions (or 'redds') into which eggs are laid and then fertilized during the winter months. Most members of the salmon family undertake upstream spawning migrations, or else seek out well-flushed lake margins, moving up to suitable spawning sites from deep lakes (the Arctic Charr), lower reaches of rivers (Brown Trout) or the sea (Sea Trout and Atlantic Salmon). Once they reach their destination, male fish establish and then vigorously defend spawning territories over optimal gravels.

The single exception to this pattern of winter spawning amongst the salmon family is the Grayling, which instead lays its eggs on gravel in the spring. All of Britain's other freshwater fish species (except the Burbot which is now considered Extinct in the British Isles) also spawn in the spring or (often in the case of Dace and Pike) late winter, using a diversity of spawning habitats and strategies. For species such as Chub, Barbel and Tench, which are at the northern extreme of their distribution in the British Isles, spawning may be delayed until mid-summer when the water has warmed sufficiently.

Spawning substrates can range from flushed gravels generally in shallow water (used, for example, by Dace, Chub and Barbel, which also undertake upstream migration), to submerged aquatic vegetation that may also include tree roots (for species such as Roach, Common Bream and Rudd), or hard surfaces such as rocks and submerged tree boughs (for example Perch and Ruffe). Males of both British freshwater species of stickleback build nests of vegetation into which they attract mates to lay their eggs, the male then caring for the brood until the fry are free-swimming and able to disperse to fend for themselves. Males of the highly territorial Bullhead attract females to lay their eggs on the roof of the 'caves' under the stones, rocks or woody debris that they inhabit, driving off the females after spawning and caring for the eggs and hatchlings until the fry become free-swimming.

However, most British freshwater fishes exhibit no brood care once the eggs are laid, relying on the production of a large number of eggs to ensure that sufficient individuals survive to reproductive age.

The first free-living life-stage after hatching from the egg is known as the alevin. Alevins are characterized as still being connected to a yolk sac, which they consume over a matter of weeks (for winter-spawning fishes) or days, with the body generally still curled at least for the first few days. When the yolk has been consumed and the young fish become free-swimming, they are then known as fry. Fish fry grow progressively on a diet of small aquatic organisms, generally algae and microscopic invertebrates such as rotifers, eventually becoming big enough to feed on larger invertebrates. The point at which the fry stage ends is largely arbitrary, with fish continuing to grow into their adult life-stage. During this, often long, transition they may exploit a range of habitats within river and lake systems. 'Nursery habitat', which warms quickly in the summer, supports a diversity of suitable food items and provides refuge from strong currents and predators, is particularly important for the growth and survival of juveniles.

Major exceptions to this life-strategy include the European Eel, which undertakes a reverse migration to sea to spawn in an amazing life-cycle that is assumed (but has not yet been proven) to include migration back to the Sargasso Sea, from where developing larvae (leptocephali) are known to drift back on ocean currents to repopulate European waters. The estuarine species (three species of mullet, European Seabass, Flounder and Sand-smelt) spawn in coastal waters, although estuaries may be important nursery areas, whereas the Smelt (also known as the Sparling) spawns in estuaries that provide important habitats during all its life-stages.

The life-cycle of the Atlantic Salmon

Illustration by Robin Ade, reproduced courtesy of The Atlantic Salmon Trust.

Habitats for freshwater fishes

Freshwater fishes inhabit a wide range of aquatic habitats from flowing to standing water, fresh to brackish, deep to shallow, and open to well-vegetated. Some species are resilient and hardy enough to survive in virtually any watercourse or water body. Notably, these include the Three-spined Stickleback and the European Eel, as well as the Roach, which occurs in almost all aquatic habitats ranging from duck ponds to main rivers, and from salmon rivers to estuaries. Both the eel and the stickleback can even survive in the sea, as well as in relatively polluted fresh waters. The European Eel can also sometimes be found in turbulent headwaters of rivers where the Three-spined Stickleback and Roach do not fare well.

The species richness of freshwater fishes in Europe, distributed by HydroSHED basins (major hydrological drainage basins).

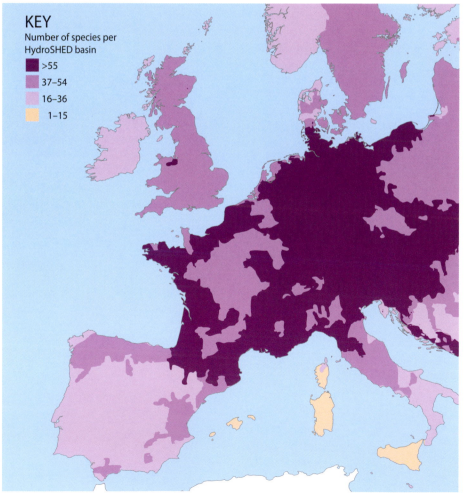

KEY
Number of species per
HydroSHED basin
- >55
- 37–54
- 16–36
- 1–15

After Freyhof, J. and Brooks, E. (2011) European Red List of Freshwater Fishes. Luxembourg: Publications Office of the European Union.

Map of Britain and Ireland showing some of the major rivers, freshwater lakes and water bodies.

Pentland Firth

The Minch

Dornoch Firth

Moray Firth

Cromarty Firth

Little Minch

Findhorn

Spey

Deveron

Don

Dee

SCOTLAND

Sea of the Hebrides

Tay

ATLANTIC OCEAN

Forth

Loch Lomond

Firth of Forth

GLASGOW

EDINBURGH

Clyde

Tweed

Firth of Clyde

Nith

NORTH SEA

Solway Firth

Tyne

Wear

Eden

Tees

Foyle

Bann

NORTHERN IRELAND

Lough Neagh

BELFAST

Upper Lough Erne

Lagan

Strangford Lough

Bann

Lower Lough Erne

Erne

Lake District

Lune

Swale

Ure

Derwent

Ribble

Wharf

Aire

Lough Conn

Shannon

Lough Mask

Lough Ree

Boyne

IRISH SEA

MANCHESTER

Lough Corrib

Liffey

DUBLIN

LIVERPOOL

Mersey

REPUBLIC OF IRELAND

Shannon

Lough Derg

Trent

Witham

The Wash

Nore

Barrow

Dee

WALES

Cardigan Bay

BIRMINGHAM

The Fens

Nene

The Broads

Suir

Trent

Great Ouse

Blackwater

Teme

Severn

Lee

Teifi

Avon

ENGLAND

Wye

Usk

St George's Channel

BRISTOL

Thames

LONDON

CARDIFF

Bristol Channel

Avon

Medway

Arun

Tamar

Strait of Dover

ENGLISH CHANNEL

13

Riverine habitats

A view held widely since the 1950s is that European rivers comprise a sequence of zones. One of the most popular river classifications was published by Marcel Huet in 1959. This identified five major ecological zones based on the longitudinal section (*i.e.* the slope of the stream bed), and the cross-section of the stream and its valley. Comparison of the relationship between these factors was used to evaluate running waters and estimate their fisheries potential, as follows:

Current speed (cm per second)	Zone descriptor	Features
> 90	Fishless	Too turbulent for fish
> 60	Trout zone	Trout with Bullhead, Minnow and Stone Loach
> 20	Grayling zone	Grayling and faster-water species including Dace, Gudgeon and Bleak
> 10	Barbel zone	Barbel typifying moderate currents shared with fish such as Chub, Dace and Bleak
< 10	Bream zone	Dominated by shoals of bream and other deeper-bodied fish, including smaller species such as Gudgeon and Bleak

The Bristol Avon, north Wiltshire: a lowland clay river, ideal habitat for Roach, Chub, Perch and Pike.

In reality, this approach is too simplistic for classifying the diversity of river systems, both in their natural state and when substantially modified by humans. For example, although many rivers and river tributaries that rise on lower and flatter land have slow flows, they are dominated by small, well-vegetated channels that are too small to sustain species such as Common Bream. In such situations, the term 'bream zone' is therefore somewhat redundant.

Today, river habitats are thought of as a continuum: the faster and slower, and shallower and deeper reaches merging with each other, influenced by geology, topography, hydrology and localized natural features. These factors are augmented by human modifications such as weirs, channel straightening and bank reinforcement, as well as flood embankments and other infrastructure that disconnects channels from floodplains. Nevertheless, the concept of different zones of rivers suiting different species, particularly differentiating habitat best suited to fish of the salmon family and other river species, remains valid. However, in reality, describing river zones is complex due to the often small-scale mosaic of microhabitats. For example, Brown Trout may thrive along with Minnow and Chub in the faster, better-oxygenated waters immediately

The River Otter in Devon, a flashy, short river running from the Blackdown Hills, populated by Sea Trout, Brown Trout and Brook Lampreys, with mullets and European Seabass occupying the estuary.

below a weir on a lowland river whilst, perhaps as little as half a kilometre downstream, shoals of deeper-bodied fish such as Common Bream and Roach may inhabit the deeper and slower flows above the next weir.

High-gradient streams running from hard geology are typical habitat for species such as trout, Bullhead, Minnow and Stone Loach. Other less streamlined and less well-adapted species are unable to survive in such conditions.

As flows decline at lower gradients, rivers may broaden as more tributaries feed into them, forming wide floodplains. These are often rich in wetland habitats, suiting the needs of many different species of plants, fishes and other animals, as well as a diversity of their life-stages. Backwaters, marginal open water, well-vegetated fringes and a range of other wetlands provide important spawning and nursery habitats for fish and are the prime habitat for smaller species such as Spined Loach. When the connection with other wetland habitats is lost, so too is much of the ecological diversity and character of the river.

The headwaters of many river systems and their tributaries arising in low-gradient landscapes may be substantially influenced by intensive farming or may be otherwise heavily managed. Frequently, over-management reduces these watercourses to little

The River Wye, Powys: a fast-flowing river flowing over a steep topography of bedrock, classic habitat for Atlantic Salmon, Brown Trout, Grayling and lampreys, and a river in which Allis Shad and Twaite Shad spawn.

more than ditches. Yet ditches can be important habitats for fish and other wildlife, particularly species such as the Three-spined and the Ten-spined Sticklebacks and the Spined Loach, which may fare less well in big open waters where there are many competitors and potential predators. Large fenland and other drainage ditches are an enlarged version of this form of slow or still water habitat. Over-management of habitat, land drainage and other related practices, and pollution, together with the impacts of introduced species of fishes and other animals and plants, are just some of the threats facing freshwater fish species in British and Irish rivers and stillwaters.

Estuarine habitats

As rivers meet the sea, they naturally broaden into wide estuaries, often with the formation of tidal mudflats and saltmarshes. In the upper, fresher-water regions of this estuarine zone, shoals of Common Bream, Roach and other deeper-bodied fishes, as well as their predators, may prosper. In saltier lower reaches, visitors from the sea such as mullet, European Seabass, Flounder and Smelt may be more common. Habitat loss through urban and agricultural encroachment may substantially change the character of this estuarine zone, including its biodiversity and many beneficial functions such as the provision of natural sea defences.

The Taw Estuary, north Devon: a broad estuary with intertidal mudflats, providing habitat for mullets, Flounder, European Seabass and Sea Trout.

Still waters

The standing waters of the British Isles are also diverse, ranging from large glacial lakes through to lowland meres and small, weeded and sometimes temporary farm ponds. Waters that dry out intermittently are populated by fish with resilient life-stages (generally eggs) in many other countries, but not in the British Isles. The fish-free status of these waters may make them important habitats for amphibians, water beetles and other, sometimes scarce, aquatic life. Insensitive 'rehabilitation' of these temporary ponds, including digging them out and stocking the now permanent water with fish, can adversely affect their conservation value. However, small, weeded ponds holding permanent water may be important habitat for species such as Crucian Carp and Ten-spined Stickleback, which are able to survive in poor water quality. In such ponds they are able to evade open water species of fish with which they generally do not compete well. Silver Bream, Rudd, Perch and Roach can also thrive in small duck ponds, dew ponds, marshes and other enclosed water bodies, Rudd and Perch in particular often breeding profusely but forming stunted populations.

The large glacial lakes of north-west England, Wales, Scotland and Ireland provide deep, cool conditions suitable for scarcer species including the Arctic Charr and the whitefishes. These fishes are under considerable threat from nutrient enrichment and organic pollution from sewage inputs and run-off from adjacent farmland. These factors tend to depress the oxygen concentration of the deeper waters in

Llyn Cwellyn in Gwynedd, Wales. The deep and cool waters of upland glacial lakes may contain relict populations of Arctic Charr and whitefish (Vendace or European Whitefish), and support Atlantic Salmon and Brown Trout.

A lowland lake in north Wiltshire, habitat for Tench, Common Carp, Roach and Perch.

A well-vegetated small farmland pond in north Wiltshire, supporting Three-spined Stickleback and Rudd.

which these fish spend much of their lives, except when they are spawning in tributary streams or lake margins. Introductions of fish such as Ruffe and Roach are also threatening successful breeding of some whitefish and Arctic Charr populations.

Some man-made still waters, including gravel pits and reservoirs, can be very productive fish habitats. Many older gravel pits fed by groundwater have matured into habitat-diverse waters that support mixed fish populations. Reservoirs are often managed for both water storage and recreation, including angling, and are typically stocked with Brown Trout and the non-native Rainbow Trout. Large freshwater reservoirs can also provide excellent habitat for large predatory fish such as Pike, smaller predatory fish such as Perch, and a host of other fish species that thrive in still water.

The canal network is also populated by a wide range of fish species. Waterways such as the Kennet and Avon Canal are well interconnected with rivers and, as a consequence, have flowing water in many stretches that support riverine species such as Barbel and Chub. Many other canals are mainly still water habitats favoured by species such as Common and Silver Bream, Tench and Common Carp. When neglected, and used little or not at all for navigation, canals progressively silt up and infill but can provide rich habitats for water plants and birds, as well as fishes that favour still water and dense vegetation, such as Rudd, Crucian Carp, Ten-spined Stickleback and Spined Loach.

Man-made reservoirs may contain natural or stocked Brown Trout and/or Rainbow Trout, as well as populations of Perch and other coarse fish species.

Mature gravel pits typically hold populations of Tench, Common Bream, Roach, Rudd, Perch and Pike.

Canals, particularly those falling into disuse, can support a diverse fish population including Common Bream, Roach, Perch, Pike and European Eel.

How to identify fishes

The key to learning how to identify any group of animals or plants is first to gain a good appreciation of the commoner species. This holds true for freshwater fishes and the key features to look for are summarized in this section.

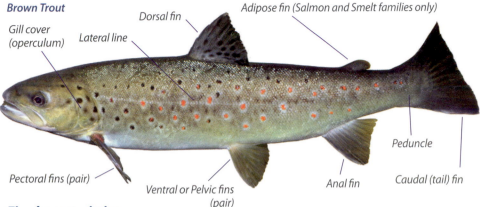

Brown Trout

Dorsal fin

Adipose fin (Salmon and Smelt families only)

Gill cover (operculum)

Lateral line

Peduncle

Pectoral fins (pair)

Ventral or Pelvic fins (pair)

Anal fin

Caudal (tail) fin

Fin characteristics

The dorsal, tail/caudal and anal fins are single, and primarily provide lateral stability and propulsion. The pectoral and ventral/pelvic fins are paired and assist with fine orientation, with the pectorals also often being used for slow 'paddling' swimming.

Some freshwater fishes have a single dorsal fin, whilst others have two (and sometimes more in the case of some fishes of the sea and of fresh waters in other countries). If there are two dorsal fins, at least for British freshwater species, the first is held erect by hard spines. The two dorsal fins may run into each other (as in the Ruffe) or be separate (as in the closely related Perch).

The leading edge of soft fins is commonly supported by a cluster

*The single dorsal fin of a Roach showing the spine (**blue text**) and soft ray (white text) count.*

III

II

I

1 2 3 4 5 6 7 8 9 10

The Perch has two separated dorsal fins (left), whereas the Ruffe's two dorsal fins merge into one (right).

22

of fused spines, with soft, branched rays supporting the rest of the fin. The spines are counted in Roman numerals, whereas soft rays are counted in Arabic numerals. As an example, the spine and ray count of the Roach dorsal fin is III/9. The spine and ray count of the dorsal and anal fins is a particularly helpful visual feature that distinguishes otherwise broadly similar fish species. For example, Common Bream have very much longer anal fins than Roach, with a correspondingly greater number of fin rays. (Beware of the rearmost rays that tend to branch close to the base, and can confuse counting.)

The orientation of fins with respect to each other can sometimes be an important diagnostic feature. For example, the leading edge of the dorsal and ventral fins of the Roach line up with each other (this is ascertained by tracing upwards along a column of scales from the base of the ventral fins to the base of the dorsal fin to account for the fact that the shape of the body may change as the fish grows), whereas the dorsal fin of the Rudd is typically set back about three scale columns with respect to the ventral fins (see *page 56*).

Scales and lateral line

Fish scales may be large and prominent, fine and less obvious, apparently absent, or completely lacking. The lateral line is a row of pressure-sensing organs running along the flanks and perforating the scales along the body. The lateral line may be complete, running as far as the tail, or may stop short. Counting the number of scales along the lateral line, as well as noting the extent of the line, can be helpful in distinguishing similar fish species.

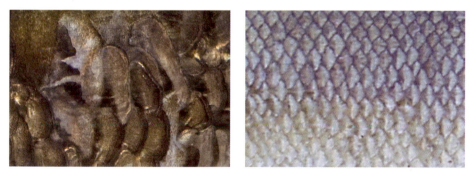

ABOVE: *The large scales of the specially bred 'Mirror' form of Common Carp (left) are very prominent; those of the Barbel (right) are much smaller.* BELOW: *The lateral line of the Bleak (left) runs all along the flank, whereas that of the Sunbleak (right) is short, finishing towards the tip of the pectoral fin.*

The streamlined body shape of the Dace (top) contrasts with the deep-bodied profile of the Common Bream (bottom).

Dace

Common Bream

Body shape

Some fish such as Common Bream are deep-bodied and laterally compressed, sometimes giving large specimens the nicknames of 'dinner plates' or 'dustbin lids'. This is an adaptation to stable swimming in still or slow-moving waters, enabling intricate orientation by the fish to feed on small food items buried in muddy beds (primarily chironomid larvae, known as 'bloodworms').

By comparison, fish such as trout and Dace are streamlined in profile and have a rounded cross-section, adapting them to life in faster flows in open water. Barbel, too, are well streamlined, but the body is flattened beneath better suiting them to life on the river bed.

The swim bladder and buoyancy

Although the swim bladder it is not a feature used in everyday identification, it has considerable bearing on fish behaviour. The swim bladder is formed by an outgrowth of the gut, comprising an air sack that adjusts buoyancy. Some species, such as eels and loaches, lack a swim bladder. Perch and similar 'advanced fishes' possess a swim bladder that is sealed and is therefore inflated and deflated with pneumatic glands. However, fishes of the carp and minnow family (the cyprinids) lack these glands. Consequently, the swim bladder has to be 'topped up' by gulping air from the surface, or by releasing bubbles if the fish needs to become less buoyant. This is why cyprinid species such as Roach or Bream are commonly seen 'priming' at the surface, often at dusk. This is generally as a prelude to feeding in shallower, food-rich waters where they may be vulnerable to predation during daylight hours.

Mouth and barbels

The mouth of a fish may be 'superior' (opening upwards as in the Bleak, centrally located (as in the Dace) or 'inferior' (underslung as in the Barbel). The position and size of the mouth gives an indication of where the fish may feed.

The mouth of the Barbel is surrounded by two pairs of strong barbels, or 'whiskers'. These are fleshy and chemically sensitive appendages that assist the fish in searching for food on the river bed. A small Barbel may sometimes be confused with a large Gudgeon but a key distinguishing feature is that Gudgeon have a single pair of small barbels, one at each corner of the mouth. Many species, such as the Dace, lack barbels.

Some fish, such as Pike and Zander, have particularly strong teeth to enable them to catch live prey. Others, including all of the carp and minnow family (the Cyprinidae), lack teeth along their jaw. However the cyprinids have powerful teeth deep in their throat, which are in fact modified gill rakers used to crush hard food items including shells and seeds. These throat, or pharyngeal, teeth are important distinguishing features for closely related and hybridized fish, but the fish has to be killed to dissect them out: this requires considerable expertise and is beyond the scope of this guide.

FROM TOP TO BOTTOM: *The Bleak has an upward-oriented mouth that adapts the fish well to feeding from the surface.*

The mouth of the Dace is centrally located, enabling the fish to intercept food drifting in the current, as well as from the river bed and water's surface.

An inferior (underslung) mouth, surrounded by strong, fleshy barbels (or 'whiskers') equips the Barbel to feed on the river bed.

The capacious mouth of the Pike is armed with strong teeth to trap live prey.

Bleak

Dace

Barbel

Pike

The types of fishes

This section provides an introduction to the types of fishes that are native or have been introduced into British and Irish fresh waters. The 53 species concerned include representatives from 21 families, including a number that are not truly freshwater residents but can be found in estuaries and lower reaches of rivers, mainly during summer months. An example from each of these families is shown here (approximately to scale) with a brief description of key distinguishing features. Each is cross-referenced to the relevant section of this guide that contains the individual species account(s). The descriptions of key features of these fishes are based only on the species found in the fresh waters of the Britain and Ireland.

A Brown Trout swims over the gravel bed of a clear river, essential habitat for salmonids to spawn successfully.

Carp and minnow family (Cyprinidae)

Pages 52–79

19 British species (12 native; 7 introduced)

All cyprinids lack stomachs, have toothless jaws, bodies covered evenly by scales that may be conspicuous or small (with the exception of some scaleless artificially reared strains), and have a single dorsal fin supported by soft rays behind fused spines at the leading edge.

The cyprinids range in size from the Sunbleak and Topmouth Gudgeon (11 cm / 4 inches) to the Common Carp (up to 110 cm / 43 inches).

Rudd

Gudgeon

Common Bream

Salmon, trout, charr, freshwater whitefish and grayling family (Salmonidae)

Pages 80–93

8 British species (7 native (from 2 sub-families), 1 of which is Extinct; and 1 introduced). Other species have been introduced historically, but have not become established.

These fishes are slender and streamlined with pelvic fins set far back on the underside and a fleshy adipose fin towards the rear of the back. The mouth contains a single row of sharp teeth. They range in size from the European Whitefish (46 cm / 18 inches) to the Atlantic Salmon (up to 150 cm / 59 inches).

Grayling

Herring, shad, sardine and menhaden family (Clupeidae)

Pages 111–112

2 British species (both native marine species that spawn in freshwater rivers)

The body of the British shads is strongly laterally compressed and generally herring-like. The head is scaleless, but the body is covered by large, round and smooth scales. The teeth are small or minute. Mature shads range in size from 60 cm / 24 inches in the case of the Twaite Shad to 69 cm / 27 inches in the case of the Allis Shad.

Twaite Shad

Pike family (Esocidae) *Pages 94–95*

1 British species (native)

Pikes have large mouths armed with strong teeth adapted to a predatory lifestyle. The tail fin is forked and the dorsal and anal fins are set well back on an elongated body, enabling rapid acceleration. Pike can grow to 130 cm / 5 feet in length.

Pike

3 British species (2 native; 1 introduced from mainland Europe)

Fishes in this family possess two dorsal fins, the anterior of which has strong spines, with the posterior supported by soft rays and either separated from or contiguous with the anterior dorsal fin. They range in size from the Ruffe (at 20 cm / 8 inches) to the Zander (at up to 100 cm / 39 inches) in length.

Perch

Stickleback and tubesnout family (Gasterosteidae)   *Pages 114–116*

2 British species (both native)

The bodies of these small fishes are generally elongated and lack scales, or are covered by scutes (large bony scales) along the sides. The mouth lacks barbels and is generally small, at the end of a narrow tapering snout. There are a number of well-developed dorsal spines in front of the dorsal fin. The two species are similar in size at 11 cm / 4 inches when mature.

Sculpin family (Cottidae)   *Pages 106–107*

1 British species (native)

The body of the Bullhead appears scaleless, though there are prickles on the gill cover and elsewhere. The eyes are set high on the head. These bottom-dwelling fishes live under stones and lack a swim bladder. They grow to 18 cm / 7 inches in length.

Bullhead

River loach (or hillstream loach) family (Balitoridae)

Page 104

1 British species (native)

These loaches have elongated bodies with small, inferior mouths surrounded by at least three pairs of barbels. Stone Loach grow to 13·5 cm / 5·5 inches in length.

Loach family (Cobitidae)

Page 105

1 British species (native)

These fishes have a spindle- or worm-like body with a small, inferior mouth surrounded by at least three pairs of barbels. There is a characteristic erectile spine beneath each eye. Mature Spined Loach are just 12 cm / 5 inches in length.

Hake and burbot family (Lotidae)   *Pages 109–110*

1 British species (native but now considered extinct)

These cod-like fishes possess two dorsal fins, a single anal fin and a rounded tail fin, as well as a single chin barbel. Burbot grow up to 152 cm / 5 feet in length.

Black Bullhead

North American freshwater catfish family (Ictaluridae) *Page 102*

1 British species (introduced from North America)

The head has eight barbels – two on the snout, two maxillary and four on the chin. The body is scaleless and has an adipose (fatty) fin towards the rear end of the back. The Black Bullhead can grow to 66 cm / 26 inches in length.

Burbot

Sheatfish catfish family (Siluridae)

Pages 100–101

1 British species (introduced)

The body is elongated, lacks obvious scales, and tapers behind a large mouth. There are no barbels on the snout, but one or two pairs on the lower jaw; an elongated pair of maxillary barbels is also present. The eyes are small and widely spaced. When mature, they can be up to 5 m / 16 feet in length.

Sturgeon family (Acipenseridae)

Pages 108–109

1 British species (native; predominantly marine but spawns in freshwater rivers)

The body is elongated and armed on the sides by five rows of scutes, or large armoured scales. The mouth is small, inferior and toothless, and there are four small barbels in front. Mature individuals can attain 6 m / 20 feet in length.

Common Sturgeon

Brook Lamprey

Lamprey family (Petromyzontidae)   *Pages 119–123*

3 British species (all native, 2 of which have a marine life-phase)

The body is eel-like with a cartilaginous skeleton, and lacks scales and paired fins. The mouth lacks jaws, comprising simply a circular disk. Larval forms, known as ammocoetes, are characterized by a line of circular gill openings behind the eye. They range in size from the Brook Lamprey (at 20 cm / 8 inches) to the Sea Lamprey (up to 120 cm / 47 inches).

Freshwater eel family (Anguillidae)

Pages 117–118

1 British species (native; breeds at sea and migrates to coastal and fresh waters)

The snake-like body is covered in minute scales coated in a thick layer of slime. The dorsal fin is contiguous with the caudal and anal fin. Mature individuals are up to 91 cm / 36 inches in length.

Sunfish family (Centrarchidae) *Page 103*

1 British species (introduced from North America)

The body is laterally compressed and rounded in profile. There are two dorsal fins, the anterior of which is supported by strong spines. They grow to 20 cm / 8 inches in length.

European Eel

Righteye flounder family (Pleuronectidae)

Page 126

1 British species (native; mainly marine but penetrates up rivers, mainly in the summer)

The body is flattened with both eyes normally on the right side of the head. The fins lack spines, including the dorsal fin, which extends onto the head. The upperside of the body is pigmented, whilst the underside is white. Flounder grow up to 30 cm / 12 inches in length.

European Seabass

Temperate bass family (Moronidae)

Page 127

1 British species (native; mainly marine but may penetrate up rivers, particularly in the summer)

There are two dorsal fins, the first supported by strong spines; the second with a single anterior spine behind which are 10–13 soft rays. There are also two spines on the rear of the gill cover. European Seabass can grow to 60 cm / 24 inches in length.

Mullet family (Mugilidae)

Pages 128–129

3 British species (native; mainly marine but penetrate up rivers, particularly in the summer)

Mullets possess two dorsal fins: the first short, supported by four stout spines; the second soft and well-separated. The pectoral fins are placed high on the flanks. The upward-oriented mouth has rubbery lips and usually lacks teeth, although sometimes small teeth may be present. They range in size from the Golden Grey Mullet (at 50 cm / 20 inches) to the Thick-lipped Grey Mullet (at up to 75 cm / 30 inches).

Thin-lipped Grey Mullet

Smelt family (Osmeridae)

Page 125

1 British species (native; estuarine)

The body is streamlined and silvery in colour, and the mouth is large and armed with both premaxillary and maxillary teeth. Smelt grow to 30 cm / 12 inches in length.

Smelt

Silversides family (Atherinidae)

Page 124

1 British species (native; estuarine)

The body is silvery, elongated, laterally compressed and covered in relatively large scales. These fishes have two widely separated dorsal fins, the first with flexible spines and the second with one spine followed by soft rays. Sand-melt grow to 20 cm / 8 inches.

Sand-smelt

Glossary and technical terms

Acidification occurs when acidified rainfall increases the acidity of water as the buffering capacity of local soils is overwhelmed. Although acidification is a natural process, contributing to the often acidic character of many naturally mineral-poor upland ecosystems, the term 'acidification' is more commonly associated with atmospheric pollution. Mineral-poor upland areas downwind of pollution sources, such as upland streams and other ecosystems in mid-Wales, are particularly vulnerable to acidification, which may have profound effects on fish and other wildlife.

The **adipose fin** is a small, soft and fleshy fin composed of fatty tissue, located between the dorsal and caudal (tail) fins of fishes of the salmon and smelt families (and some other fish families that are not native to British fresh waters).
The function of the adipose fin remains a mystery, though it is believed to have sensory functions.

Alevins are newly hatched juvenile fish still attached to the yolk sac. The term is particularly used for juvenile stages of salmon and trout when the alevins lie where they hatch in the **redd** consuming the yolk before venturing out into the water column as free-living **fry**.

Ammocoete. The larval stage of species of lamprey (see *pages 119–123*).

Anadromous. A fish that lives in the sea but returns to fresh water to breed, for example the Atlantic Salmon, Sea Trout or lampreys.

The **anal fin** is located on the lower surface of the body of a fish, between the anus and the caudal fin (see *page 22*). In some fishes, such as eels and lampreys, the anal fin is contiguous with the **caudal fin**. The anal fin stabilizes the fish whilst swimming.

BAP. The UK Biodiversity Action Plan (UK BAP) (see *page 135*).

Barbels, sometimes also referred to as 'whiskers', are slender and tactile, whisker-like organs around the mouth and/or on the snout of some fishes. (Barbels are sometimes mistakenly called barbules.)

The **adipose** fin of a Brown Trout.

Common, particularly in the catfish, carp and some other families, barbels are generally densely covered with chemical sense organs and are used to sense potential food (see *page 25*).

Basking. During sunny and still weather, fish such as Common Carp and Chub tend to bask in the warmer upper surface layer of the water column, intermittently loafing, cruising and sometimes feeding from the surface film.

Benthic. The benthic zone is the level of a body of water closest to and including the sediment surface and sub-surface. Animals and plants living here are known as benthic organisms.

Carnivorous. Animals that consume a diet of (predominantly) animal matter, either vertebrates or invertebrates.

Catadromous. A fish that lives in fresh waters but returns to the sea to breed, for example the European Eel.

Catch-and-release is a conservation practice in recreational angling in which fish are unhooked once caught and returned alive to the water (see *page 137*).

The **caudal fin** is also known as the tail fin (see *page 22*), and is found at the end of the body, often located on a caudal **peduncle**. Caudal fins come in a variety of shapes, and may be forked, blunt-ended or rounded. In some fishes such as eels and lampreys, the caudal fin is joined with the **dorsal fin** and the **anal fin**.

The **closed season** is a statutory period during which angling and/or commercial fishing is banned for stock protection purposes; in fresh waters this is generally during spawning (see *page 136*).

A **coarse fish** is, in a British freshwater context, one that is not a member of the salmon family. (According to some definitions, the Grayling, although a member of the salmon family, is classified as a coarse fish owing to the spring timing of its spawning, hence angling for Grayling being prohibited during the coarse fish **closed season**.)

*The **barbels** of a Common Carp.*

Detritus is generally defined as non-living particulate organic material. It may be abundant in slow-moving and still water bodies, as well as slack margins and interstices in faster-moving rivers. It forms particularly through decomposition of plant matter and faecal matter. Micro-organisms may comprise a substantial component of detritus, meaning that some fish (such as Roach), as well as many invertebrates, utilise it as food.

The **dorsal fin**, or fins, is (or are) located on the back of the fish (see *page 22*). Whilst some fish families can have three dorsal fins, the British freshwater fishes have either one or two (excluding the fatty 'adipose fin' of the salmonids), the front one containing more spines and the rear one supported by soft rays. Dorsal fins are not paired, provide vertical stabilization and assist in turns and stops.

An **endemic** species is one that is unique to a defined geographic location.

The term **epiphytic** describes plants, animals or films of microorganisms that grow on the surface of aquatic vegetation.

Eutrophication is a consequence of nutrient enrichment of water bodies, increasing their productivity and standing biomass. In lakes, 'blooms' of algae are a common consequence of eutrophication, potentially depleting oxygen concentrations as organic matter decomposes. This particularly threatens deep-water species such as Arctic Charr and the whitefishes, amongst a range of other negative impacts on ecology and human uses of water.

Filter-feeding is the habit of straining suspended food particles from water, typically in fish by passing the water over modified **gill rakers**. The **ammocoete** larval stage of Brook and River Lampreys, which can account for most of the life-span of the species, are filter-feeders. Allis Shad and Twaite Shad (though also being opportunist predators) tend to filter-feed on plankton at sea, and this capacity for filter-feeding is reflected in the structure of their numerous, long **gill rakers**.

Fins are surfaces used by fish for stability and/or to produce lift, thrust or steerage in water. In bony fish, most fins may have **rays** and often also **spines**.

Fry is a term used to describe early juvenile free-swimming life-stages of fishes, when the juveniles are reliant upon external sources for nutrition. In salmon and trout, the fry is the life-stage between **alevin** and **parr**. For many species, young fish are generally considered fry during their first year, although the term is somewhat imprecise.

A **game fish** is, in a British freshwater context, a member of the salmon family (noting the status of the Grayling as discussed under '**coarse fish**'.)

Gills are the respiratory organs of fish, allowing the inward diffusion of dissolved oxygen and outward diffusion of carbon dioxide and other waste matter between water and blood. Gills consist of thin filaments of tissue with a highly folded surface, arranged on **gill arches** supporting them in a flow of water at the back of the mouth, through which fine blood vessels flow. The vulnerability of the gills means that they are armoured with **gill covers**, which also assist with respiration.

Gill arches (or branchial arches) are a series of bony structures beneath the gill covers of fish that support the gill filaments.

The **gill cover**, or **operculum**, is a hard bony flap covering and protecting the gills in most fishes (see *page 22*).

Composed of four fused bones, the gill cover of modern bony fish appears to have evolved by the joining of gill-slit covers of ancestor species. Gill covers are vital for effective respiration, opening as the mouth closes and conversely to maintain a uniform direction of flow of oxygenated water through the gills.

Gill rakers are bony or cartilaginous projections from the **gill arches**, generally present in two rows respectively projecting from the anterior and posterior side of each **gill arch**. Aside from a protective function for the vulnerable gill tissue, the gill rakers are also involved in **filter-feeding** on tiny prey suspended in the water column. The structure and spacing of gill rakers correlates with feeding behaviour, and can be useful in identification of closely related species.

Guanine pigment imparts the reflective, silvery colour over the body surface of many fish species.

Herbivorous. Animals that consume a diet of (predominantly) plant matter, including organic detritus.

Ichthyology is the branch of the scientific study of animals (zoology) devoted to the fishes.

Inferior (mouth). See **underslung**.

An **impoundment** is an obstruction in a river that holds back water, including, for example, man-made dams and weirs, as well as natural obstructions such as log jams and other large woody debris.

A **kype** is the hooked lower jaw that develops in mature salmonid fishes prior to spawning, and which is used as a weapon to defend spawning territories and potential mates against other competing male fish.

The **lateral line** comprises a chain of pressure sensory organs along the flanks of most fish species (see *page 23*), helping them to detect movement, vibration and pressure waves in the surrounding water. The lateral line is usually visible as a line of perforations in the skin or scales along the flank. The line may be complete, running from the **gill cover** to the tail, or may be incomplete, as in the Sunbleak. The count of scales along the lateral line may be a distinguishing feature in the identification of some species, such as the 56–61 scales along the lateral line of the Orfe.

Leptocephalus (pl. leptocephali) The oceanic larval stage of the European Eel as it undertakes its two-year passive drift in the plankton from the Sargasso Sea to European shores.

Maxillary refers to the upper jaw bone; **premaxillary** relating to the region immediately above the upper jaw.

Milt is the seminal fluid of fish (and indeed of molluscs and other water-dwelling animals). Milt contains sperm and nutritious substances, and is released into the water to fertilize the eggs laid by female fish.

Minor species is a term used to group smaller species of fish that are nevertheless important members of aquatic ecosystems, some of which are of priority conservation importance.

Nursery habitat. An area of habitat suiting the needs of juvenile fish, providing refuge from predation and strong flows as well as abundant food. For many river species, rapidly warming nursery areas, typically in marginal shallows or connected wetlands, may be vital for promoting the swift growth of juvenile fish such that they grow large enough to withstand strong currents during autumn spates.

Oligotrophic refers to an ecosystem that has a naturally low level of nutrient

*A salmon **parr***

substances, for example many upland streams and large glacial lakes. The flora and fauna of these habitats, including for example Arctic Charr and whitefishes that inhabit deep but well-oxygenated regions of lakes, is adapted to oligotrophic conditions, and so is highly vulnerable to **eutrophication**.

Omnivorous. Animals that consume a varied diet comprising both animal and plant matter.

Operculum. See **gill cover**.

Overbite. In those fishes where the upper jaw extends beyond the lower jaw, and often the snout extends beyond both, there is said to be an overbite. This may form part of a range of useful distinguishing features, for example with Roach generally having a clear overbite unlike the closely related Rudd that has an upward-slanted mouth.

A **papilla** (pl. papillae) is a small protuberance on the skin, the term literally meaning 'nipple-like'.

Parr is the term used for a young salmonid fish during much of the freshwater period of its juvenile life, before it transforms into either the adult stage, or into a **smolt** for species that take to sea as adults. Parr are characterized by 'parr bars', a series of dark, parallel markings along their sides (see *page 83*).

The **pectoral fins** are paired and are located on each side of the body, generally just behind the **gill covers** (see *page 22*). These fins are used for 'paddling' and delicate orientation, as well as for lift and maintaining depth in currents.

The large pectoral fins of bullheads may be used for securing the fish onto a river bed or in its home cave. Pectoral fins, as indeed all paired fins, are absent in the lampreys.

Pelagic. The pelagic zone is open water that is neither close to the bottom nor near the shore. Animals and plants living here are known as pelagic organisms.

Pelvic fins. See **ventral fins**.

Peduncle. The caudal peduncle of many species of fish is the narrow part of the body, generally tapering in width, to which the tail attaches (see *page 22*).

Pharyngeal teeth (or 'throat teeth') are found in the throat of fishes of the carp and minnow family (Cyprinidae), which lack teeth in the jaw or mouth (as well as in some other fish families occurring outside the British Isles). Pharyngeal teeth are modified from **gill arches** and are used to crush or grind hard food items. In some species, grinding of the pharyngeal teeth can be used to make a sound. The shape of the pharyngeal teeth may be used definitively to identify some fish species or their hybrids, but requires the fish to be killed.

*Roach have a clear **overbite**.*

Piscivore. A carnivorous fish or other animal that primarily eats fish.

Planktivore. A fish or other animal that feeds primarily on plankton, or small organisms suspended in the water column. Most British planktivorous fish species eat zooplankton (small animals such as water fleas) rather than phytoplankton (small plants mainly comprising algae). Plankton is an important part of the diet of the **fry** of many small fishes.

Pores. Spaces, including both those found in gravel beds into which fish eggs may fall, or else pits through fish scales.

Priming. The action of a fish breaking the water's surface in order to gulp air.

Rays. The **fins** of many fishes are supported by rays, which are soft, flexible and generally branched. The segmentation of rays differentiates them from **spines**.

Recruitment of fish is the addition of new juveniles to the population.

A **redd** is a spawning depression in gravel 'cut' by breeding fishes. In salmonid fishes, males migrate to and defend suitable habitat for redd digging, but it is the female that 'cuts' the redd by shimmying her body energetically before depositing eggs into the loose gravel.

Although salmonids do not generally cover the redd, further redds cut upstream by the female may cover the previous one(s). This process continues until the female is spent. Salmonid redds have a characteristic upstream depression and downstream hummock where displaced gravel is redeposited by currents. Lamprey species also form redds, groups of males and females making shallow excavations in sandy or gravely substrates by individually moving particles. A few days after collective spawning in the redd, the adult fish die.

SAC. A Special Area of Conservation, designated for the protection of species or habitats scheduled under the EU Habitats Directive (see *page 133*).

Scales. The skin of most fishes is covered by hardened bony plates known as scales (see *page 23*). Scales vary widely in size, shape, structure and extent, and can be used to identify fish families and species.

Scute(s). Large scales serving as armour on the flanks of some fishes, notably the sticklebacks.

Siltation refers to the generally undesirable increase in the amount of silt entering a watercourse. Silt has a range of adverse impacts including eutrophication of waters with associated nutrient-rich

*A spawning depression or **redd**, the paler area in this image.*

substances. It also 'blinds' sediments making them unsuitable for the formation of redds by salmonids and the growth of some water plants, as well as blanketing the gaps beneath stones that are used by species such as bullheads.

Smolt. For salmonid fishes with sea-going adult life-stages, the smolt is the phase into which the **parr** metamorphose on migration to estuaries before taking fully to the sea. Smolts lose their 'parr bars' and take on a silvery colouration.

Spines. Many fishes have spines as well as soft **rays** to support the **fins**. Spines are generally stiff and sharp but are sometimes flexible and always unsegmented. Aside from stiffening **fins**, or often just the leading edge of **fins** in front of branched **rays**, the spines in some species are used as a form of defence, or may help fish lock themselves into crevices. Perch and some other fish also have spines on the rear of the **gill covers**.

The **spine and ray count** is the number of spines (usually counted in Roman numerals) and soft rays (counted in Arabic numbers) supporting a **fin** (see *page 22*). Spine and ray counts of the **dorsal fin** and

anal fin can be useful features supporting identification of fish species. For example, the spine and ray count of the long **anal fin** of the Common Bream is III/24–30.

'Springer' is a shorthand term for a spring salmon, one that returns from the sea to run rivers early in the year. Springers are often larger specimens.

Stunting. Inhibition of growth of animals as a result of overcrowding or other poor environmental conditions; commonly found in populations of Perch, Rudd or Crucian Carp that have bred profusely in small ponds.

The **swim bladder** (or gas bladder or air bladder), is an internal gas-filled sac enabling fish to control their buoyancy, offering them the advantage of maintaining their swimming depth. The swim bladder also serves as a resonating chamber increasing the ability of the fish to detect sounds (see *page 24*).

Tail fin. See **caudal fin**.

Throat teeth. See **pharyngeal teeth**.

Triploid is the term used for fish with three sets of chromosones, instead of the more usual pair (diploid). Although

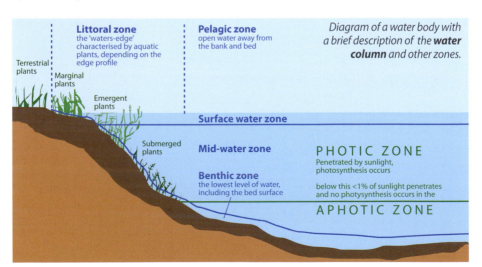

Littoral zone
the 'waters-edge' characterised by aquatic plants, depending on the edge profile

Pelagic zone
open water away from the bank and bed

Terrestrial plants

Marginal plants

Emergent plants

Submerged plants

Surface water zone

Mid-water zone

Benthic zone
the lowest level of water, including the bed surface

Diagram of a water body with a brief description of the water column and other zones.

PHOTIC ZONE
Penetrated by sunlight, photosynthesis occurs

below this <1% of sunlight penetrates and no photysynthesis occurs in the

APHOTIC ZONE

*A male Minnow in breeding dress with white **tubercles** on the head and **gill cover**.*

appearing and behaving much as diploid fish, triploids are sterile as they do not develop normal eggs or sperm and are unable to breed. Natural triploids are known to occur, but commercial production of triploid trout, usually by shocking eggs with pressure or heat, means that the fish grow quicker in aquaculture and do not reproduce or cross-breed when released or if they escape into the wild.

Tubercles are small, rounded swellings that develop on many fish species, particularly males in the carp and minnow family (Cyprinidae), as a prelude to spawning. They develop most densely around the head and front of the body and are believed to provide tactile stimuli that promote the release of eggs by females and to aid the male's adhesion to the female's flank when releasing **milt**.

Underslung (mouth). For those fish species in which the mouth has a pronounced downward orientation below the snout, such as Barbel, the mouth is said to be underslung (or '**inferior**' – see *page 25*).

The **ventral** (or pelvic) **fins** are paired and located ventrally below the **pectoral fins** but before the anus (see *page 22*). The ventral fins help the fish maintain orientation in the water, turn and stop. Ventral fins are vestigial in the European Eel and are absent in the lampreys.

Vomerine teeth are small teeth that are found on the front part of the roof of the mouth in some species, such as the European Seabass.

Water Column. The depth profile vertically through a body of water that typically comprises a surface water zone, a mid-water zone (open waters away from the shores of the water body are known as the pelagic zone) and a benthic zone adjacent to the bed.

*The **vomerine teeth** of a Pike.*

Salmon watching

KEY

1. Falls of Shin, Sutherland – River Shin
2. Glen Tanar Estate, Aboyne, Aberdeenshire – River Dee
3. Falls of Feugh, Banchory, Kincardineshire – River Dee
4. Rocks of Solitude, Edzell, Angus – River North Esk
5. Pitlochry Dam and Salmon Ladder, Perthshire – River Tummel
6. Cargill's Leap, Blairgowrie, Perthshire – River Ericht
7. Buchanty Spout, Easter Glenalmond, Perthshire – River Almond
8. Larbert Weir, Stirlingshire – River Carron
9. Philiphaugh Salmon Viewing Centre, Scottish Borders – River Ettrick
10. Hexham Weir, Northumberland – River Tyne
11. Stainforth Foss, Yorkshire – River Ribble
12. Lydford Gorge, Devon – River Lyd
13. Cenath Falls, Ceredigion – River Teifi
14. Lovers' Retreat, Camowen, Tyrone – River Camowen

An Atlantic Salmon leaping upstream is an amazing sight. It can be observed during peak migration periods, typically in rising river conditions during late autumn or early winter, where fish encounter obstacles to their upstream progress, such as weirs. Locations in the UK where this is a frequent sight under the right river conditions are shown on this map. For more information, visit The Atlantic Salmon Trust website (see *page 139*).

The species accounts

The species accounts in this book are grouped by family, and arranged as far as possible so that species that appear similar are grouped together. This means that the order of species is not strictly taxonomic (a summary of this order is given in the Contents pages at the beginning of the book). Throughout the species accounts, the text is cross-referenced to other parts of the book as appropriate, although page references to species that are on adjacent facing pages have been omitted.

Species that have been introduced are shown on pages with a pale red background.

Tables summarizing the identification features for similar species are included in the relevant accounts, with key features highlighted in bold.

Distribution maps have generally not been included in the species accounts due to the incomplete knowledge of the range of most species, and the extent of introductions.

Both metric and imperial measurements are given, with the notation " being used for 'inches' in the body text.

A consistent approach is adopted for each species account, as explained below:

English name

Other names: Alternative and other (often local) names used for the species.

A general summary of the species' distribution, life-strategy, key aspects of behaviour, food preferences and other relevant information.

Identification: A brief description and summary of the key identification features.

Ecology: Details of habitat preferences, breeding biology and other ecological aspects.

Conservation: A summary of the species' fisheries and/or nature conservation interests.

1. **IUCN Red List category** (see *page 132*).
2. **Bern Convention** (see *page 133*).
3. **Habitats Directive** (see *page 133*).
4. **Native or introduced to Britain.**
5. **UK Biodiversity Action Plan Priority Species** (see *page 135*).
6. **Wildlife and Countryside Act 1981** (see *page 135*).
7. **The Import of Live Fish (England and Wales) Act 1980** (see *page 136*).
8. **Prohibition of Keeping or Release of Live Fish (Specified Species) Order** (see *page 136*).
9. **Status in Britain and Ireland**: summary.
10. **Habitat(s) in which found**: summary.
11. **Maximum recorded length and weight in Britain.**

Scientific name

The scientific (usually Latin) name generally used for the species, and in some cases the former name where the name has changed.

Summary of status, legislation and protection

1	**IUCN Red List category**
2	**Bern Convention (App. II or App III)**
3	**Habitats Directive (Ann. II, IV or V)**
	Native
4	**Introduced, Naturalized**
	Introduced, Invasive
5	**UK BAP Priority Species**
6	**W&C Act (Sched. 5)**
	W&C Act (Sched. 9)
7	**ILFA Import restriction**
8	**Prohibition Order**
9	**Common and widespread**
10	**Habitat: Riverine, Still Water &/or Estuarine**
11	**Max. length:** 150 cm (59 inches)
	Max. weight: 29 kg (64 lb)

A summary of the key identification features, with cross-references to similar species.

Carp and minnow family
Cyprinidae

19 British species
(12 native; 7 introduced)

The Cyprinidae, also known as cyprinids, is the largest family of freshwater fish globally, with over 2,400 species in about 220 genera across North America, Africa and Eurasia.

The cyprinids lack stomachs and have toothless jaws, though hard food items are crushed with pharyngeal (throat) teeth formed from modified gill rakers, which can also be used by specialists to identify species. Some cyprinids possess barbels. There is only one dorsal fin supported largely by soft rays but with generally three fused spines supporting the leading edge. The cyprinids possess a well-developed swim bladder, used to adjust buoyancy, which is charged by gulping air and discharged through the mouth and gut. Many cyprinids have prominent scales, but others have small scales and may appear scaleless. (However, the 'leather carp' form of the Common Carp may be entirely lacking in scales.) The key features that help to distinguish the cyprinids found in the British Isles are summarized in the table below.

Cyprinids have a varied diet, with most species feeding predominanly on invertebrates and vegetation, due largely to their lack of teeth and a stomach, although some species are predatory.

Summary of the distinguishing features of Britain's cyprinids

Species	Page	Native or introduced	Barbels	Scales
Rudd	54	Native	Absent	Conspicuous
Roach	55	Native	Absent	Conspicuous
Orfe	57	Introduced, locally naturalized	Absent	Conspicuous
Chub	58	Native	Absent	Conspicuous
Dace	59	Native	Absent	Conspicuous
Common Bream	60	Native	Absent	Conspicuous
Silver Bream	62	Native	Absent	Conspicuous
Barbel	63	Native	Two pairs	Conspicuous
Tench	64	Native	One pair	Small
Crucian Carp	66	Native	Absent	Conspicuous
Goldfish	67	Introduced, locally naturalized	Absent	Conspicuous
Common Carp	70	Introduced periodically since 15th century, widely naturalized	Two pairs	Conspicuous (or rarely absent)
Grass Carp	72	Introduced, non-breeding, locally established	Absent	Conspicuous
Gudgeon	73	Native	One pair	Conspicuous
Minnow	74	Native	Absent	Very small, apparently scale-less
Bleak	76	Native	Absent	Conspicuous
Sunbleak	77	Introduced, invasive, locally naturalized	Absent	Conspicuous
Topmouth Gudgeon	78	Introduced, invasive, locally naturalized	Absent	Conspicuous
Bitterling	79	Introduced, locally naturalized	Absent	Conspicuous

*This hybrid **Roach × Common Bream** shows characteristics of both species, such as the relatively long anal fin, smaller and more numerous scales and dark fin colours of the bream, yet the smaller head and more delicate mouth of the Roach.*

Cyprinid identification is complicated by the tendency amongst some closely related species, such as Common Carp, Goldfish and Crucian Carp, to interbreed. However, it is amongst the 'dace-like' fishes (sub-family Leuciscinae) that the greatest confusion tends to arise. The potential for hybridization between these species, including the introduced Orfe, is summarized in the following table. This guide does not go into detail about hybrid identification (except where noted under species descriptions); hybrids tend to have characteristics that are intermediate between the parent fish species, although they are variable.

Rudd	Yes						
Silver Bream	Yes	Yes					
Common Bream	Yes	Yes	Yes				
Chub	Rarely	No	No	No			
Dace	No	No	No	No	No		
Bleak	Rarely	No	Rarely	Rarely	No	No	
Orfe	No	No	No	No	No	Rarely	No
SPECIES	**Roach**	**Rudd**	**Silver Bream**	**Common Bream**	**Chub**	**Dace**	**Bleak**

Body shape	Scales along lateral line	Spines/rays in dorsal fin	Spines/rays in anal fin
Deep and laterally compressed	40–45	III/8–9	III/10–11
Deep and laterally compressed	42–45	III/9–11	III/9–11
Streamlined and round in cross-section	56–61	III/8	III/9–10
Streamlined and round in cross-section	44–46	III/8–9	III/7–9
Streamlined and round in cross-section	48–51	III/7	III/8
Deep and laterally compressed	51–60	III/9	III/24–30
Deep and laterally compressed	44–48	III/8–9	III/21–23
Streamlined and flattened underneath	55–65	III/7–9	III/5
Oval and round in cross-section	Many small scales	III/8	III/6–78
Deep and laterally compressed	32–25	III–IV/14–21	III/6–8
Deep and laterally compressed	28–33	III–IV/15–19	II–III/5–6
Deep and laterally compressed	35–40	III–IV/17–22	II–III/5
Streamlined and round in cross-section	40–42	III/7–8	III/7–11
Streamlined and flattened underneath	38–44	III/5–7	III/6–7
Streamlined and round in cross-section	Lateral line incomplete	III/7	III/6–7
Streamlined and laterally compressed	48–55	III/8–9	III/16–20
Streamlined and round in cross-section	Incomplete lateral line with about 8–12 pored scales	II–III/7–9	III/10–13
Streamlined and round in cross-section	34–38	III/7	III/6
Deep and laterally compressed	34–38	III/9–10	III/8–9

Rudd

Scardinius erythrophthalmus

Other names: None

Rudd are found primarily in standing waters, although they can also thrive in slow-flowing rivers. They are generally found in the middle and upper layers of water, often cruising and feeding at the surface in warm weather. Young rudd feed extensively on small invertebrates, such as water fleas and aquatic insects, but become increasingly omnivorous as they mature.

Identification: Rudd have a deep body profile, large, conspicuous scales over a generally golden-silver body colour, and crimson fins. The mouth lacks teeth and barbels. Mature Rudd in good quality water with rich food sources can have a particularly deep golden hue and vivid crimson fins. However, in enclosed waters this species is prone to 'stunting', resulting in a general lack of bright colouration.

Rudd commonly hybridize with Roach, but also Silver Bream (*page 62*) and Common Bream (*page 60*), particularly where these shoal-spawning species occur together due to a lack of optimal habitat.

Ecology: Rudd require the same submerged vegetation habitat as Roach to spawn and, like Roach, they spawn in shoals from April to June, depending on conditions. There is no parental care. They grow slowly, at about the same rate as Roach, but tend to occupy more

Least Concern
Native
Common and widespread
Still Water

Max. length:	50 cm (20 inches)
Max. weight:	1·8 kg (4 lb)

Rudd are most often confused with Roach but are distinguished by the following features:

- Lateral line scale count.
- Dorsal fin spine and soft ray count.
- Anal fin spine and soft ray count.
- Base of first spine of dorsal fin **set back** 2–3 scale columns relative to the ventral fins.

See table on *pages 52–53* for details.

open areas of water, where they feed at and just below the surface.

Conservation: In addition to good water quality, Rudd require a variety of aquatic habitats if they are to thrive. This provides a diversity of food items and, as with the Roach, good habitat complexity enables them to evade predators and increases the availability of food-rich warm water where young fish can maximise their rate of growth in the summer. Submerged stands of vegetation, such as the underwater stems of emergent plants, are also essential for successful spawning.

Roach

Rutilus rutilus

Other names: None

The Roach is one of the most widespread species of freshwater fish in Britain and Ireland. It is found in standing and flowing waters, usually in the middle and lower layers, but will cruise and feed nearer the surface in warm weather. It is omnivorous, juveniles feeding extensively on small invertebrates and algae and older fish tending towards a more plant- and detritus-based diet.

Identification: Roach have a deep body profile, large and conspicuous scales over a generally silver-coloured body and bright red fins. The mouth lacks teeth and barbels.

Roach will hybridize with Rudd, Silver Bream (*page 62*), Common Bream (*page 60*) and, rarely, Chub (*page 58*), particularly where spawning habitat is impoverished and the shoals are forced to spawn together. Hybrids tend to have intermediate characteristics between the parent fish.

Ecology: Roach spawn in shoals on submerged vegetation from April to early June, depending on conditions. There is no parental care. The young are slow growing and require both warm summer conditions and heated marginal shallows to enable them to grow large enough to survive autumn/winter spates. Peak growth rate during their first summer can be as much as 30% of their body

Least Concern	
Native	
Common and widespread	
Riverine, Still Water, Estuarine	
Max. length:	50 cm (20 inches)
Max. weight:	1·8 kg (4 lb)

Roach are most often confused with Rudd and Silver Bream (*page 62*), but are distinguished by the following features:

- Scale count along the lateral line. Spines and soft rays on the dorsal fin.
- Spines and soft rays on the anal fin.
- Leading edge of dorsal fin **in line** with that of ventral fins (counting up the scale columns).

See table on *pages 52–53* for details.

weight per day, with juveniles reaching 5–7 cm (2–3") after one year and 10–15 cm (4–6") by their third. Roach breed after three years (exceptionally two) and can live for 15 years or more. They prefer to stay in marginal waters, unlike Rudd, which are more often found in areas of more open water.

Conservation: Good water quality and quantity are important for the Roach, but so too is a complexity of habitats. Diverse habitat supports a wide variety of food items, enabling the fish to evade predators, and provides

food-rich marginal water that warms quickly and maximises the growth of young fish in the summer. A diverse range of spawning habitats inhibits hybridization owing to reduced competition for scarce habitat with other species. Submerged vegetation, particularly water mosses such as species of *Fontinalis*, but also other aquatic plants including the underwater stems of reed stands, is important for successful spawning. Areas of deep water are particularly important for Roach during the winter.

Rudd *Base of first spine of dorsal fin set back 2–3 scale columns relative to the ventral fins.*

Scale count along the lateral line 40–45 (this individual = 42)

Roach dorsal fin spine and soft ray count

Roach *Leading edge of dorsal fin in line with that of ventral fins (counting up the scale columns)*

Scale count along the lateral line 42–45 (this individual = 42)

Differentiating features of Rudd and Roach

Feature	Rudd	Roach
Scale count along the lateral line	**40–45**	42–45
Spines and soft rays on the dorsal fin	**III/8–9**	III/9–**11**
Spines and soft rays on the anal fin	**III/10–11**	III/**9**–11

Orfe

Leuciscus idus

Other names: Golden Orfe, Ide

The Orfe is not native to the British Isles but has been widely introduced to the wild as a result of releases from the ornamental fish trade. It is found naturally across continental Europe and Asia in fresh (occasionally brackish) slowly flowing and still waters. Adult Orfe tend to be solitary, feeding primarily on larger invertebrates and fish fry at all depths of the water column. Juveniles are gregarious and feed on algae and small invertebrates.

Identification: Orfe have relatively small but conspicuous scales over a silvery body colour, paler beneath and darker on the back in its natural colour form, although a 'golden' form, which is a popular introduction to garden ponds, is better-known. The outer edges of the dorsal and anal fins are convex, and the tail is forked. The mouth lacks teeth and barbels.

Orfe are not known to hybridize with British native species, although examples of hybrids with Dace (*page 59*) have been very rarely reported from continental Europe.

Ecology: Orfe thrive in good water quality with adequate flow, and where a variety of habitats provide them with an abundant and diverse range of food. They require deep waters for overwintering and shallow areas for spawning. In north-western and central Europe, Orfe undertake migrations to tributaries where they spawn communally in

Least Concern	
Introduced, Naturalized	
Localized	
Riverine	
Max. length:	85 cm (33 inches)
Max. weight:	4 kg (8·8 lb)

Orfe are most often confused with Dace (*page 59*) and sometime small Chub (*page 58*), but are most simply distinguished as follows:

- The outer edges of the dorsal and anal fins of Orfe and Chub are convex, whilst those of Dace are concave.
- Orfe have many more smaller scales (**56–61** along the lateral line) compared to Dace (48–51) and Chub (44–46).

April and May in moderate current on gravel or submerged vegetation. The sticky eggs generally attach to submerged vegetation or clean gravel surfaces. There is no parental care. Insect larvae constitute the main food items throughout the life of the fish, although other invertebrates are also eaten.

Conservation: Orfe populations have naturalized in some British waters, for example in the River Mole in Surrey, but are not generally widespread other than through releases from overstocked aquaria and ponds. Where populations of Orfe do become established, they could potentially be a significant threat to native fishes.

Chub

Squalius cephalus

Other names: Chevin, Loggerhead

Chub are common fish of flowing waters, although they can survive and grow large (though not breed) in big standing water bodies, and can live for 20 years. This is an omnivorous species equipped with a large mouth that engulfs anything in its path – whether animal or vegetable. Although juveniles feed on algae and small invertebrates, older fish become increasingly omnivorous as they grow, predating fish, amphibians and other small animals. Chub are found at all depths in flowing waters, mostly feeding on the bed, but are often seen cruising at the surface where they take emerging insects and other floating matter.

Identification: Chub have large, conspicuous scales over a brassy-coloured body. The dorsal and tail fins are dark or black, and the ventral fins tend to be reddish. The body profile is streamlined but 'chubby' and the mouth lacks teeth and barbels. Chub are known to hybridize with Roach (*page 55*), although very rarely, but not with other species of fishes.

Ecology: Chub spawn in shoals in river gravels in late spring. Spawning depends on warm weather and is often deferred until mid-summer and it is not uncommon for chub to fail to spawn at all in cooler summers, reflecting the fact that Britain is towards the northern extent of the species' range.

Least Concern	
Native	
Common and widespread	
Riverine	
Max. length:	60 cm (24 inches)
Max. weight:	6·7 kg (10 lb)

Chub are most often confused with Dace, but can be distinguished readily by the outer border of the dorsal and anal fins: those of Chub are convex; those of Dace are concave.

There is no parental care. In rivers, fry require warm, shallow marginal water to enable them to grow quickly enough to withstand the winter spates that, following cool summers, can kill off most of that season's juveniles. As a consequence, Chub populations commonly contain just a few strong year classes of fish.

Conservation: Chub do not especially require unpolluted water, but good water quality and quantity enable them to thrive. A varied habitat is important as this provides an abundant and diverse range of food, refuges in which to overwinter, well-flushed gravels for spawning, and places to evade predators (such as cormorants and Pike). Young fish need food-rich warm water, generally in the river margins, to maximize their growth in the summer.

Dace

Leuciscus leusciscus

Other names: Dare, Dart

The Dace is a common fish of flowing waters and is found at all depths feeding primarily on invertebrates. It is often seen at the surface taking drifting and emerging insects, particularly in the summer months. Caddisfly (Trichoptera) larvae are particularly significant prey items. Juveniles feed on algae and small invertebrates, but older fish become more carnivorous, including taking fish fry.

Identification: Dace have large, conspicuous scales over a silvery body, pale fins, and a slender and streamlined body profile. The mouth lacks teeth and barbels.

The Dace is not known to hybridize with other native species, even those that are closely related, perhaps due to its tendency to spawn early in cool waters. Very rare examples of hybrids with Orfe (*page 57*) are known from continental Europe.

Ecology: Dace spawn in shoals on submerged gravels early in the year (February to May depending on the conditions). There is no parental care. This adaptation to spawn early in the year enables juvenile Dace to exploit the spring 'explosion' of productivity in river systems. Adaptation to cool conditions also enables Dace to feed and grow throughout the year and, as a consequence, the 'growth rings' on the scales of Dace are less distinct

Least Concern	
Native	
Common and widespread	
Riverine	
Max. length:	40 cm (16 inches)
Max. weight:	0·6 kg (1·5 lb)

Dace are most often confused with Chub, but can be distinguished readily by the outer border of the dorsal and anal fins: those of Dace are concave; those of Chub are convex. Orfe could possibly be a confusion, though this species also has a convex anal fin and also has many more smaller scales (**56–61**) along the lateral line compared to Dace (48–51).

than those of species in which growth slows significantly during the winter months.

Conservation: Dace thrive in good quality water with adequate flow, and where a varied habitat provides them with abundant and diverse food items. Deep areas of water are important for overwintering, with shallow, well-flushed gravels necessary for spawning. Good habitat complexity also enables Dace to evade predators such as cormorants and Pike. Young fish require food-rich warm water, generally in the river margins, to maximize growth during the summer.

Common Bream

Abramis brama

Other names: Bream, Bronze Bream

Common Bream is a shoaling species that is widespread in standing and slow-flowing waters. They have an omnivorous diet, and are particularly well-adapted to grubbing up chironomid (bloodworm) larvae from soft silt. Young fish feed extensively on small invertebrates, whereas older fish tend towards a more varied diet. This species commonly occurs in the lower layers of water, feeding on the bed of the river or lake.

Identification: The Common Bream has large, conspicuous scales. The body colour is silvery in younger fish but darkens to deep bronze with age, and the fins are dark. The body profile is very deep and laterally compressed, and the mouth lacks teeth and barbels. This laterally flattened body shape explains the nickname 'dustbin lids' often used to describe large Common Bream and the nickname 'skimmers' commonly used to describe smaller specimens.

Common Bream commonly hybridize with Roach (*page 55*), and sometimes also with Silver Bream (*page 62*) and Rudd (*page 54*). Hybrids occur most frequently where shoals are forced together due to a lack of otpimal spawning habitat. The hybrids possess intermediate features (including scale counts on the lateral line and fin spine and ray counts).

Ecology: Common Bream spawn in shoals on submerged vegetation during May or June depending on the conditions. There is no parental care. This species grows slowly and requires a range of habitats from vegetated

Least Concern
Native
Common and widespread
Riverine, Still Water, Estuarine

Max. length:	82 cm (32 inches)
Max. weight:	9 kg (20 lb)

Common Bream are most often confused with Silver Bream (*page 62*), but can be distinguished by the following features:

- Lateral line scale count.
- Dorsal fin spine and soft ray count.
- Anal fin spine and soft ray count.
- The mouth can be protruded into a tube to aid feeding in silt (unlike Silver Bream).

See table below for details.

shallows through to silt-bedded deeper water, the former for spawning and nursery areas and the latter for refuges and feeding as adults.

Conservation: Common Bream are not especially exacting about water quality, often prospering in enriched waters that have relatively low oxygen levels. Varied habitat provides this species with diverse food items, deep areas for overwintering, and habitat complexity to evade predators such as cormorants and Pike. However, juveniles are found in shallower, marginal waters that are food-rich and that warm quickly, enabling them to maximize growth during their first summer. Submerged stands of vegetation, including underwater stems of reeds, are necessary for successful springtime spawning.

Differentiating features of Common Bream and Silver Bream

Feature	Common Bream	Silver Bream
Scale count along the lateral line	51–60	44–48
Spines and soft rays on the dorsal fin	III/9	III/8–9
Spines and soft rays on the anal fin	III/24–30	III/21–23

A male showing
spawning tubercles
on the head.

Common Bream ▲   ▼ Silver Bream

Silver Bream

Blicca bjoerkna

Other names: White Bream, Bream Flat

Found in standing and slow-flowing waters, Silver Bream commonly occur in the lower layers and feed on the bed of the river or lake. Young fish feed extensively on small invertebrates and older fish tend to have a more omnivorous diet.

Identification: The body of the Silver Bream is deep and laterally compressed, with large, conspicuous scales. They have small heads with a moderate hump where it joins the body. The body colour is silvery in younger fish and the fins are colourless, this generally silvery/grey appearance persisting into adult life. The mouth lacks teeth and barbels. The eye of a Silver Bream is very large by comparison with its head – typically one quarter of the length of the head from the tip of the snout to the posterior edge of the gill cover. This relationship changes little over the lifetime of the fish. Large eye size is an additional defining characteristic that sets the Silver Bream apart from the Common Bream (*page 60*), and all other European cyprinids apart from Bleak (*page 76*).

Silver Bream is known rarely to hybridize with Common Bream, Roach (*page 55*) and sometimes Rudd (*page 54*), the hybrids possessing characteristics that are intermediate between the parent species. Hybridization occurs most often where the spawning habitat is suboptimal and shoals of the different species are forced to spawn in the same location.

Ecology: Silver Bream spawn in shoals on submerged vegetation during May to early July depending on the conditions, and may have three or four spawning events during this period. There is no parental care. They grow relatively rapidly, reaching a length of about 9 cm (3·5") in their first year, although

Least Concern	
Native	
Locally common	
Riverine, Still Water	
Max. length:	36 cm (14 inches)
Max. weight:	0·6 kg (1 lb 5 oz)

Silver Bream are most often confused with Common Bream (*page 60*), being similar in profile, with a long anal fin, although this is not as long as that of the Common Bream. They are distinguished by the following features:

- Lateral line scale count.
- Dorsal fin spine and soft ray count.
- Anal fin spine and soft ray count.
- The mouth does not protruded into a tube to aid feeding in silt (unlike Common Bream).

See table on *page 60* for details.

growth slows thereafter. Males normally mature after their third year and females after their fourth year.

Conservation: Silver Bream require reasonable water quality, and a range of aquatic habitats is also important. Such areas provide a diversity of food items and enable these fish to evade predators. Areas of deep water are important overwintering habitat. Like Roach, Rudd and Common Bream, shallow, marginal waters that are food-rich and that warm quickly are essential for the survival and growth of early life stages. Stands of submerged and marginal vegetation are also necessary as spawning substrate.

See *page 61* for comparative images of Silver Bream and Common Bream.

Barbel

Barbus barbus

Other names: 'Whisker', 'Beard'

The Barbel is a robust river fish, but it has also been introduced to some standing waters. An omnivorous species, it inhabits the lower layers of rivers and feeds on the river bed. Although juvenile Barbel feed extensively on small invertebrates, older Barbel have a broader diet that also includes plant matter and other items that they root out from aquatic sediments using their strong and fleshy lips and barbels.

Identification: Barbel have large and conspicuous scales over a generally bronze or olive body, and amber fins. The body is sturdy and streamlined, but flattened on the underside reflecting their benthic habits. The mouth lacks teeth, but has two pairs of prominent, leathery barbels. Barbel are not known to hybridize.

Least Concern		
Native		
Locally common		
Riverine		
Max. length:		120 cm (47 inches)
Max. weight:		9 kg (20 lb)

Juveniles may be confused with large Gudgeon (*page 73*), but are distinguished by having two pairs of barbels rather than a single, smaller pair.

Ecology: Barbel spawn in shoals on well-flushed gravels during late May to the end of June depending on conditions, disturbing the gravel to enable the sticky eggs to fall into open pores. There is no parental care. The British Isles is the extreme northern extent of the Barbel's range, and as spawning requires

Adult Barbel (above) are robust and streamlined; juveniles (below) often have mottled colouration.

warm weather it may not occur at all in some cooler summers. The young are slow-growing, dependent upon warm summer conditions and heated marginal shallows to grow big enough to evade autumn/winter spates.

Conservation: Barbel require good water quality and flows. Habitat diversity is also important, including well-flushed, open gravels for spawning; deep areas

for overwintering; good marginal habitat complexity to provide refuges; and rapidly warming, food-rich nursery areas particularly for juveniles. Varied habitat also supports diverse food items, as well as helping the fish evade predators such as Pike, cormorants and otters. Siltation of rivers is a particular problem for spawning Barbel, as it can 'blind' sediments and consolidate and deoxygenate the gravels essential for spawning.

Tench

Tinca tinca

Other names: Doctor Fish

The Tench inhabits densely weeded still waters and river backwaters. It is an omnivorous species, juveniles feeding extensively on a range of invertebrates and algal matter and older fish feeding on the lake or river bed, where they grub for molluscs, aquatic insects and crustaceans, and plants.

Identification: Tench are characteristically olive-green, or occasionally brownish, fading to yellow beneath and with small, bright-red eyes. The scales are small and numerous, and the skin velvet-like to the touch due to a dense covering of slime. The fins are rounded, the ventral (pelvic) fins of males upward-curved and spoon-shaped; all are olive-coloured, more or less matching that of the body. The body is rounded in cross section and oval in general profile. The mouth lacks teeth but has a single downward-pointing barbel at each corner. The mouth can be protruded to aid feeding. Tench do not hybridize with other species.

Ecology: Spawning takes place on dense vegetation in rapidly warming shallows between May and exceptionally as late as July, when the water reaches 18 °C. Groups of males chase and jostle gravid females, which shed many small (<1mm), green, sticky eggs that adhere to water plants. There is no parental care. Juveniles require warm shallow water throughout the summer in order to find plenty of food and promote growth.

Least Concern		
Native		
Common and widespread		
Still Water		
Max. length:		70 cm (28 inches)
Max. weight:		6·8 kg (15 lb)

Their distinctive colour and profile means that Tench are unlikely to be confused with any other freshwater fish species.

They grow very slowly, typically reaching only 3 cm (1·2") after one year, and tend to remain cryptic, living in dense vegetation. Males typically mature after three years and females after four years.

Conservation: Tench do not require very high water quality, often surviving where oxygen dips to a low level at night. However, they do require dense vegetation as a refuge from predators and, in rivers, areas where they can shelter from strong flows.

A lack of suitable spawning and nursery habitat can be a significant contributory factor to the failure of Tench populations to perpetuate themselves in man-made waters such as gravel pits and reservoirs. Such water bodies are often steep-sided and lack dense areas of fringing vegetation and shallow warm margins required for successful breeding.

ABOVE: *The green colouration and rounded fins and body of Tench make them difficult to confuse with other species. Adult (top) and juvenile (bottom) fishes are shown above to illustrate the variation in shape and colouration.*

BELOW: *Female Tench (top) have a soft, rounded profile, adapted to bearing a large egg-mass that may comprise a substantial proportion of body weight in the spring. Males (bottom) have stronger, paddle-shaped, curved ventral fins and a conspicuous bony hump where they attach on the belly.*

Crucian Carp

Carassius carassius

Other names: Crucian, Carassin (French)

The Crucian Carp is a small, often cryptic fish found in still waters. It occurs naturally on the eastern side of England but is now more widespread due to introductions across the British Isles. It is tolerant of low oxygen conditions, thriving in densely vegetated pools and marshes. However, it competes only poorly with other species in more open waters and is invariably found near the bottom of pools, often close to the cover of vegetation.

Identification: The Crucian Carp is notably hump-backed with conspicuous scales over a brassy or sometimes olive-coloured body. The mouth lacks barbels and is far smaller than that of the Common Carp (*page 70*) with which this species can sometimes be confused. The dorsal fin is long with a strong, slightly serrated third spine before the soft rays.

Crucian Carp also interbreed with both Common Carp and Goldfish. Hybrids with Common Carp are usually betrayed by the presence of barbels around the mouth. Hybrids with Goldfish are notoriously difficult to discern, and their identification is generally best left to specialists.

Ecology: The Crucian Carp is well-adapted for life in small ponds or densely weeded pools and marshes, tolerating poor water quality and surviving well in high temperatures as well as prolonged ice cover. It may also burrow in mud during the winter. Spawning takes place from May to, exceptionally, as late as July during several, isolated, periods. Females shed their small (1·4–1·7 mm diameter) eggs into dense vegetation in shallow water, where they adhere to water plants. There is no parental care. The growth rate of juveniles varies

Least Concern
Native
Localized
Still Water

Max. length:	64 cm (25 inches)
Max. weight:	3 kg (6 lb 10 oz)

Crucian Carp can be distinguished from the Common Carp (*page 70*) by:

- The lack of barbels round the smaller mouth.
- Lateral line scale count.
- Dorsal fin spine and soft ray count.

Crucian Carp are also easily confused with Goldfish, which some authorities regard merely as a regional subspecies of Crucian Carp. They can be distinguished by:

- Lateral line scale count.
- Dorsal fin spine and soft ray count.

See table below for details.

according to habitat, but is generally slow. Both juveniles and adult fish feed on small animals and plant matter throughout their life.

Conservation: As Crucian Carp can tolerate low oxygen levels, they are well adapted to small pools, marshes and densely vegetated shallow still waters. However, they will not thrive where other fish species are present or persist where there are strong currents. Well-vegetated habitat is important, providing diverse food and refuges for all life stages.

The greatest threat facing Crucian Carp would appear to be hybridization with Goldfish, which are now widely introduced into British waters, as well as over-management of still waters robbing them of well-vegetated habitat.

Differentiating features of Crucian Carp, Goldfish and Common Carp

Feature	Crucian Carp	Goldfish	Common Carp
Barbels	none	none	two pairs
Scale count along the lateral line	32–35	28–33	35–**40**
Spines and soft rays on the dorsal fin	III–IV/**14**–21	III–IV/15–19	III–IV/17–**22**

Goldfish

Carassius auratus

Other names: None

The Goldfish is a small fish native to the still waters of central Asia, China and Japan, which has been introduced widely across the world, including to the British Isles, mainly as a consequence of deliberate releases from the ornamental fish trade. It can live for up to 60 years. When wild populations of Goldfish revert to their natural, bronze colour form, they appear very similar to Crucian Carp; indeed, some authorities consider Goldfish to be just a regional subspecies of the Crucian Carp. Goldfish inhabit the bottom of pools, often close to vegetation.

Identification: Like Crucian Carp, Goldfish are notably hump-backed with conspicuous scales over a brassy or sometimes olive-coloured body in the natural form. However, varieties with orange or other colours are found in ornamental strains, which may also have highly modified body and fin shapes.

Goldfish also interbreed with both Crucian Carp and Common Carp (*page 70*). Their hybrids have intermediate features and can be notoriously difficult to identify.

Ecology: Goldfish, like Crucian Carp, are well adapted for life in small ponds or well-vegetated pools and marshes, and are able to tolerate poor water quality. For this reason, they are particularly suited as ornamental fish in garden ponds and aquaria. They do not thrive in waters where there are strong currents.

Spawning takes place when the water temperature exceeds 20°C, the small, sticky eggs adhering to water plants. There is no parental care. Juvenile and adult fish feed on small animals and plant matter throughout their life, the growth rate of juveniles varying according to habitat. The high temperature required for spawning may mean that Goldfish reproduce inefficiently in the wild in Britain, and sustained populations are probably a result of repeated introductions

Conservation: The most significant conservation issue is the threat that the widely introduced populations of Goldfish pose to native populations of Crucian Carp, mainly due to the impact of hybridization. In addition, the introduction of Goldfish to previously fish-free ponds can disrupt the ecosystem balance and threaten invertebrate and water plant populations.

Not evaluated	
Introduced, Naturalized	
Locally common	
Still Water	
Max. length:	32 cm (13 inches)
Max. weight:	1·8 kg (4 lb)

Goldfish and Crucian Carp are very hard to tell apart, although Crucian Carp can sometimes be distinguished by:

- Lateral line scale count.
- Dorsal fin spine and soft ray count.

Goldfish are distinguished from Common Carp (*page 70*) by:

- The lack of barbels around the smaller mouth.
- Lateral line scale count.
- Dorsal fin spine and soft ray count.

See table on facing page for details.

See *pages 68 & 69* for comparative images of Crucian Carp and Goldfish

Crucian Carp in its preferred well-vegetated still water habitat (below) with a DNA-tested pure specimen (above).

Goldfish in its preferred still water habitat (below) with a DNA-tested pure specimen (above).

Common Carp

Cyprinus carpio

Other names: King Carp, Koi, Leather Carp, Mirror Carp

The Common Carp is one of the largest and most widespread freshwater fishes found in the British Isles, and can live for up to 40 years. It is a species of still waters and larger, slow-flowing rivers. Introduced into British waters from at least the 15th century (its natural range encompasses the Black, Caspian and Aral Sea basins in eastern Europe and Asia), Common Carp have also been distributed widely around the world, largely through aquaculture, owing to their hardiness, omnivorous habits and efficient conversion of food into body mass. It is often found on or near the bed of pools and rivers, but will rise to the surface where it can commonly be seen cruising on sunny days, feeding on insects and other floating matter.

Identification: Owing to their widespread exploitation for aquaculture, ornamental fish-keeping and angling, Common Carp have been bred in a variety of forms and colours. In its natural form, the species is high-backed but elongated with large, conspicuous scales over a brassy-coloured body. Many variants have a far deeper body profile (so-called 'King Carp'), whilst others have reduced numbers of enlarged 'mirror' scales ('Mirror Carp') and some lack scales entirely or almost entirely ('Leather Carp'). Koi Carp, bred for their bright colours, occur in all forms. The fins are large, and the dorsal fin is single and elongated. Two pairs of short barbels surround the mouth, which may be protruded to aid feeding.

Common Carp may also interbreed with Crucian Carp (*page 66*) and Goldfish (*page 67*). Although the hybrid progeny possess intermediate features, they are generally betrayed by barbels, often small, around the mouth and a slightly shorter dorsal fin than Common Carp.

Ecology: Common Carp may be gregarious or solitary. They spawn on dense vegetation in rapidly warming shallows from May to, exceptionally, as late as July, when the water reaches 18–20 °C. Male fish chase and jostle

Vulnerable (wild strain)	
Introduced, Naturalized	
Locally common	
Riverine, Still Water	
Max. length:	110 cm (43 inches)
Max. weight:	27 kg (60 lb)

Common Carp can sometimes be confused with both Crucian Carp (*page 66*) and Goldfish (*page 67*). Distinguishing features include:

- The two pairs of barbels round the mouth, which can be protruded.
- Lateral line scale count.
- Dorsal fin spine and soft ray count.

See table on *page 66* for details.

gravid females, which shed many small (1·25–1·5 mm) eggs that adhere to water plants. There is no parental care. The young grow rapidly in warm water reaching 12–13 cm (4·5–5") in their first year, but take three or four years to mature. This species has an omnivorous diet throughout its life-cycle.

Conservation: Common Carp are robust fish that do not especially require unpolluted water. However, where the water quality is good and there is a sufficient quantity of food, they will often thrive. Varied habitat provides them with abundant and diverse food items, refuges in which to overwinter, and vegetated shallows for spawning and for juveniles to grow and evade their predators. Young fish require food-rich warm and shallow water to maximize growth in the summer. Larger carp may be vulnerable to predation by otters in some locations.

Like many fishes introduced beyond the natural range within which they have evolved, Common Carp can be problematic. Their large size, voracious appetites and fast growth rates, allied with their strength and hardiness, has led to their widespread introduction for aquaculture and recreational angling. However, these traits also mean that escaped or released stock can disrupt ecosystems, often profoundly so.

Owing to selective breeding for ornamental and aquaculture purposes, there are many forms of Common Carp, including the more natural fully-scaled form (above) and the 'Mirror Carp' characterized by few large 'mirror' scales (below).

Grass Carp

Ctenopharyngodon idella

Other names: White Amur

The native range of the Grass Carp is from China to eastern Siberia. It occurs in lakes, ponds, pools and backwaters of large rivers across a wide temperature range (0° to 38°C), including brackish waters, but prefers large, slow-flowing or standing water bodies with vegetation. It was introduced to the British Isles initially to control aquatic weeds, owing to its herbivorous diet, though some stocking still continues for ornamental and angling purposes. Since the species is now known not to breed in British waters, it only persists through stocking.

Identification: The body of the Grass Carp is cylindrical and elongated with prominent scales. It has an overall bronze to olive colour fading to paler below. The snout is short and the mouth is terminal, without barbels or teeth. Grass Carp are not known to hybridize.

Ecology: Grass Carp are known to spawn on river beds with very strong currents and at relatively high temperatures of 20–30°C (rarely 15°C) but have not been recorded as doing so in the British Isles. The eggs are slightly heavier than water and drift downstream suspended by turbulence – dying if they sink to the bottom. This need for very long rivers to complete the life-cycle, as well as the preferred

Not evaluated	
Introduced, Non-breeding	
ILFA Import restriction	
Localized	
Still Water	
Max. length:	150 cm (59 inches)
Max. weight:	45 kg (99 lb)

The Grass Carp may be confused with the elongated 'wild' form of the Common Carp (*page 70*) or with Chub (*page 58*). However, the Grass Carp lacks the barbels in Common Carp, and has 40–42 scales along the lateral line (44–46 in Chub and 35–40 in Common Carp).

temperature range, may be factors in the failure of Grass Carp to breed in British rivers.

They feed largely on aquatic plants and submerged grasses, but also consume detritus, insects and other invertebrates.

Conservation: Grass Carp are considered a pest in many countries to which they have been introduced due to the damage they cause to submerged vegetation. Although this has not proved to be an issue in the British Isles, where populations appear to exist due to continual stocking, caution is required in all introductions.

Gudgeon

Gobio gobio

Other names: 'Trent Barbel', Goby

The Gudgeon is a small, bottom-dwelling, bottom-feeding fish widely distributed throughout the British Isles. It shoals in suitable flowing waters, though may also abound in some standing waters. Juveniles feed extensively on small invertebrates and algae, and older fish feed opportunistically on the river bed on a range of small food items including insect larvae, worms, crustaceans and occasionally fish eggs, sucked in with the aid of lips that can be protruded.

Identification: Gudgeon have prominent scales, generally silvery in colour but mottled with spots and with an iridescent overlay. The body is streamlined, rounded in cross-section but flattened beneath, reflecting the benthic nature of their lifestyle. The fins are colourless but have some dark mottling. The mouth lacks teeth, but possesses a single pair of barbels. Gudgeon are not known to hybridize with other species.

Ecology: Gudgeon spawn communally between mid-April and July, generally when the water temperature approaches 15 °C. At this time, the head and front of the body of the male becomes densely covered in spawning tubercles. Spawning takes place often in very shallow water, with females depositing between 1,000 and 3,000 eggs on

Least Concern	
Native	
Common and widespread	
Riverine, Still Water	
Max. length:	20 cm (8 inches)
Max. weight:	140 g (5 oz)

A large Gudgeon may sometimes be confused with a small Barbel (*page 63*), although that species is generally far more robust and has two pairs of longer barbels around the mouth. Gudgeon may also appear superficially similar to the Stone Loach (*page 104*) and Spined Loach (*page 105*), but are more robust fish with prominent scales, have only a single pair of barbels, and frequent open water rather than hiding under stones or in vegetation.

stones or plants, at intervals over several days. There is no parental care. Gudgeon are not especially long-lived, although 6- and 7-year-old fish have be found.

Conservation: Gudgeon require good water quality and a variety of habitats providing a diversity of food and places to evade their many predators, which include predatory fish and piscivorous birds. Juvenile Gudgeon prosper in warmed, food-rich, shallow margins of rivers, maximizing their growth during the summer.

Minnow

Phoxinus phoxinus

Other names: None

Minnows are the archetypal 'tiddlers'. They proliferate in suitable flowing waters, particularly along the margins, but may also be found in large bodies of standing fresh water, particularly where marginal gravels are well flushed by waves. Minnows are an omnivorous species, juveniles feeding extensively on small invertebrates and algae, and older fish feeding opportunistically on a range of small food items including invertebrates and plant matter.

Identification: Due to their fine scales and smooth skin, Minnows give the impression that they are scaleless. The body is rounded in cross-section providing excellent streamlining. Colouration is brown on the upperparts and silver or white below, with a black line (actually a series of overlapping 'dots') along the side that runs the length of the body. The fins are small, rounded and colourless, and the mouth lacks teeth and barbels.

Ecology: Minnows spawn in shoals throughout the summer, generally from early May through to August, spawning several times during this period on marginal gravel. Males can become extremely gaudy at this time, developing white patches at their fin bases and their bodies taking on a kaleidoscope of emerald, red and gold colours. Females retain their overall silver-brown colouration. Males and females often form discrete shoals that come together to spawn. There is no parental care.

Least Concern	
Native	
Common and widespread	
Riverine	
Max. length:	14 cm (6 inches)
Max. weight:	20 g (0·7 oz)

Minnows are rarely confused with other species on close inspection, and are not known to hybridize.

Conservation: Good water quality and well-oxygenated conditions, including adequate flows, are required in order for populations of Minnows to thrive. A range of aquatic habitats provides not only the diversity of food items that these fishes require, but places to hide and evade their many predators, which include other fishes, piscivorous birds, and larger invertebrates such as water beetle larvae and water boatmen. Juvenile Minnows prosper in food-rich, warm shallow margins of rivers, where they can maximise their growth during the summer. Well-flushed marginal gravel runs are necessary for successful spawning.

Minnows play a particularly important role in maintaining the balance of aquatic ecosystems. They consume many small food items and in turn provide a valuable food source for a range of larger predators.

A male Minnow in breeding finery, showing a strong black 'chinstrap', bright patterning and white patches at the base of the fins.

Minnows are a common, shoaling species frequenting flowing fresh water as well as some larger, 'clean-water' lakes.

Bleak

Alburnus alburnus

Other names: 'River Swallow'

The Bleak is a small fish of flowing waters, found in the upper layers of rivers where it sometimes forms dense shoals. It is omnivorous and feeds primarily at the surface. Juveniles feed extensively on small invertebrates and algae, whereas older fish feed opportunistically on small food items, particularly invertebrates, borne on the current or the water's surface.

Least Concern
Native
Common and widespread
Riverine

Max. length:	25 cm (10 inches)
Max. weight:	170 g (6 oz)

A large Bleak may sometimes be confused with small Roach (*page 55*), Dace (*page 59*) or Chub (*page 58*), but Bleak are generally far more slightly built, have larger eyes, an upward-slanted mouth, and a long anal fin with III/16–20 spines and rays.

Identification: Bleak have prominent scales, generally silvery in colour, but are darker and commonly greenish on the back. The body is streamlined and laterally compressed and the large mouth and eyes are both upwardly pointing, reflecting the species' surface-feeding habit. The fins are colourless, and the base of the anal fin is particularly long. The mouth lacks teeth or barbels.

Bleak may hybridize with other cyprinid fish, including Roach (*page 55*) and Chub (*page 58*), although such hybrids are extremely rare.

Ecology: Bleak spawn in very shallow water on stones, gravel or nearby vegetation from April to June, when the water temperature has reached 15 °C. Males in spawning livery have white tubercles on the head and back, and the base of the lower fins may also be orange-tinted. Each female releases around 1,500 eggs. There is no parental care. Juveniles feed mainly upon small, planktonic animals, which also feature prominently in this species' diet throughout its life. Bleak mature in their third year, occasionally in their second, and rarely live longer than seven years.

Conservation: Bleak require generally good water quality and flows of water. They frequent open water, favouring stretches with varied habitats that provide both a diversity of food items and refuges from spates and predators such as other fish (including Perch, small Pike, trout and Chub) and piscivorous birds (particularly kingfishers and grebes). As with many species of fishes, juvenile Bleak prosper in warmed shallow margins of rivers, which are food-rich, where they can maximize their growth in the summer.

Sunbleak

Leucaspius delineatus

Other names: Belica, Motherless Minnow

The Sunbleak is a surface-feeding fish that occurs naturally in areas of Asia and Eastern Europe, favouring slow-flowing and still waters. This small and short-lived shoaling species has spread widely across Northern Europe through canal systems and releases from the aquatic trade, and possibly also as eggs stuck to water plants or as an unintended interloper when stocking with other species of fish. It is believed to have been introduced into English fresh waters from aquarium releases in Hampshire in the mid-1980s, and is now recorded from lakes, rivers and brooks across the country, particularly in southern counties, and is thought to be spreading.

Identification: The Sunbleak is bright silver in colour and can be easily identified by the incomplete lateral line that peters out shortly before the end of the pectoral fin.

Ecology: This species grows to adult size very quickly and is capable of breeding after only its first year of life. Eggs are laid in the spring and summer months in batches firmly glued to

Least Concern	
Bern Convention (App. III)	
Introduced, Invasive	
Prohibition Order	
Localized	
Riverine, Still Water	
Max. length:	11 cm (4 inches)
Max. weight:	16 g (0·6 oz)

water plants, which the males then guard to enhance the chances of survival.

Conservation: Like the Topmouth Gudgeon (*page 78*), the Sunbleak is a problematic species that can rapidly colonize new waters after introduction. In some British waters, populations have increased rapidly, out-competing native populations of young Rudd, Roach and breams. The fact that this species favours flowing waters makes control almost impossible once the species has become established.

Topmouth Gudgeon

Pseudorasbora parva

Other names: Stone Moroko or Clicker Barb

The Topmouth Gudgeon is a small fish native to cool, standing and flowing fresh waters from Japan westwards to the Amur basin. Its diet includes small insects, fish and fish eggs. Introduced into Britain through the ornamental fish trade, by 2005 Topmouth Gudgeon were thriving in twenty or more localities from Cumbria through the Midlands and Eastern England to as far south as Devon. It is continuing to spread.

Identification: This small fish has an elongated, spindle-like body covered in regular, prominent scales. The fins are compact, with no significant elongation of the base. The snout is slender and the mouth terminal and oriented upwards. There is generally a single prominent longitudinal pigmented line along the flank of the fish.

Ecology: Topmouth Gudgeon lay eggs in batches (usually adhered to stones) over the spring and summer months. Although there are relatively few eggs in each batch, these are laid throughout the year and are guarded by the male. This strategy improves fry survival and enables rapid population increase and colonization of new waters.

Conservation: The Topmouth Gudgeon is a rapidly reproducing, highly resilient and adaptable species that has been introduced

Not evaluated	
Introduced, Invasive	
ILFA Import restriction	
Localized	
Still Water	
Max. length:	11 cm (4 inches)
Max. weight:	16 g (0·6 oz)

to various parts of Europe and Asia, as well as to the British Isles. Its introduction has led to many reported negative ecological consequences and it is regarded as a pest species. It eats the eggs and competes with the fry of other species as well as degrading the habitat. These traits are exacerbated by the Topmouth Gudgeon's ability to breed when only one year old. In some circumstances, this species may totally dominate a new water within four to five years, predating the eggs and fry of native fish to such an extent that there is little chance of those species maintaining viable populations.

The Topmouth Gudgeon is classified as a non-native species in the highest-risk category under the ILFA legislation. It can only be hoped that this species can be contained before it displaces too many native species and disrupts British freshwater ecosystems.

Bitterling

Rhodeus sericeus

Other names: Bitterling Carp

Native to central and eastern Europe and adjacent Russian Republics, the Bitterling is believed to have become locally established in Britain as a result of aquarium releases in the 1920s. Now naturalized, the species has strongholds in south Lancashire, Cheshire, parts of Shropshire and some of the Great Ouse catchment, but is nowhere abundant.

Identification: The Bitterling has a deep, laterally compressed body and a short lateral line that peters out five or six scales behind the gill covers. The silver flanks contrast with the grey-green back, and there is a distinct metallic stripe extending from the middle of the flank to the base of the tail. The mouth is small, pointing forwards or slightly to the underside of the blunt snout.

Ecology: Bitterling favour densely weeded areas of small lakes, ponds and slow-flowing streams, with a strong preference for sandy or muddy bottoms that hold freshwater mussels. Spawning occurs from April to June, when males develop bright body colouration and select a mussel to which they attract a gravid female. The female deposits eggs into the mantle cavity of the mollusc via the mussel's siphon tube where they attach to the mussel's gills. The male's released sperm is drawn in by the mussel's filter-feeding action and the

Least Concern		
Bern Convention (App. III)		
Habitats Directive (Ann. II)		
Introduced, Naturalized		
W&C Act (Sched. 9)		
ILFA Import restriction		
Localized		
Still Water		
Max. length:		11 cm (4 inches)
Max. weight:		16 g (0·6 oz)

fertilzed eggs mature and hatch, safe from predators, within the mussel. The fry then leave the mussel via its siphon tube. The diet of the Bitterling is broad, including algae and other plant matter, invertebrates and detritus.

Conservation: Although Bitterling have not colonized Britain' as aggressively as some other non-native fishes, it is a potentially problematic species as it can displace other small native fishes. As a consequence, the import and keeping of Bitterling in British waters is controlled by legislation. However, it is included in the Bern Convention and the EU Habitats Directive as it is a conservation priority across its native range.

Salmon, trout, charr, freshwater whitefish and grayling family

8 British species
7 native (from 2 sub-families),
1 Extinct; 1 introduced (others possible)

Salmonidae

The salmonid fishes are slender and streamlined in outline, with pelvic (ventral) fins set far back on the underside and a fleshy adipose fin towards the rear of the back. The scales are conspicuous and the tail is forked. Salmonid mouths contain a single row of sharp teeth. Although the adult life-phase of some salmonids, including the Atlantic Salmon, can be marine, all salmonids spawn in fresh water. These are fast-swimming predatory fishes, feeding on invertebrates and smaller fish.

The whitefishes are also members of the salmon family (but in a separate sub-family, Coregoninae), as revealed by the presence of an adipose fin, although their small mouth and weak teeth separate them from the 'true' salmon and trout. They are important in many waters as food for various other game fishes, and are valuable commercial fish across much of their holarctic range. They mainly live in cold water lakes, although some species inhabit rivers and even brackish waters. Their general appearance is herring-like, with relatively large silvery scales on the body, and scaleless, relatively small heads.

Atlantic Salmon

Salmo salar

Other names: Salmon, 'King of the fishes'

The Atlantic Salmon is an iconic fish of European rivers, well known as a food and sporting species and for its extraordinary life-cycle. Adults are fast-swimming predatory fishes, feeding on invertebrates and smaller fish. They are anadromous, taking to the sea to feed throughout the adult stage but returning to fresh waters to spawn in their natal rivers. They have a high value in recreational angling, commercial fishing and aquaculture.

Identification: Atlantic Salmon possess the slender and streamlined profile that typifies their family, having evolved to swim fast and to cope with strong water flows. The dorsal fin has III–IV spines at the leading edge, supported behind by 12–14 soft rays. A fleshy adipose fin is set towards the rear of the back. The anal fin has III–IV spines and 9–10 soft rays. The pelvic (ventral) fins are set far back and the tail is forked. The scales are conspicuous and small, numbering 120–130 along the lateral line. The mouth is long and contains a single row of sharp teeth along the jaw. Adult fish have a blue-green body colour overlain with a silvery guanine coating. Although the fishes most frequently found in fresh waters usually have spots, they generally

Least Concern	
Bern Convention (App. III)	
Habitats Directive (Ann. II & V)	
Native	
UK BAP Priority Species	
Locally common	
Riverine, Estuarine	
Max. length:	150 cm (59 inches)
Max. weight:	29 kg (64 lb)

Features that distinguish adult Atlantic Salmon from large Brown/Sea Trout (*page 84*) include:

- a mouth that does not extend behind the eye;
- a lack of spots (generally) on the body below the lateral line; and
- a pronounced 'wrist' before the tail fin.

Hybrids between Brown/Sea Trout and Atlantic Salmon are not uncommon (estimated at around 7% of the British population) due to similar spawning habits; hybrid fish exhibit features that are intermediate between the two species.

Salmon parr are very similar to Brown/Sea Trout parr (see *page 83*). However, they have a habit of resting on their pectoral fins or touching the river bed rather than hanging in mid-water.

have few spots in their adult marine life-phase, none of which occur below the lateral line.

The most commonly encountered life-stage found in fresh waters is the parr. Salmon parr are elongated, sharing many features with adult fish, but lack the silvery colouration – instead being distinguished by between 8 and 12 characteristic dark, blue-violet 'dirty thumbprint' spots down the flanks. See illustration *opposite* for details of how to separate Atlantic Salmon parr from those of Brown/Sea Trout.

Ecology: Salmon eggs hatch during early spring in depressions known as redds, excavated by female fish during the previous winter's spawning in the well-flushed gravels of cool and clean upper reaches of rivers. Hatchlings, known as alevins, feed on their yolk sac for a number of weeks before emerging from the gravel in April or May and starting to grow. Parr are voracious feeders and, although often gregarious, are territorial. The duration of the Atlantic Salmon parr life-stage is highly variable, depending on the climate and river conditions. However, after anything between one and exceptionally six years, the parr head downriver, metamorphosing into smolts which, after a period of adjustment in estuaries, exit river systems for the marine adult life-phase.

Whilst Atlantic Salmon are found in most Irish, Welsh and Scottish rivers, the current distribution of the species in England has a northern and western bias, although some southern chalk rivers are also prominent salmon rivers.

They demonstrate schooling behaviour when heading off to open-sea feeding areas. Salmon typically begin their spawning migration back into fresh waters after between one and four years at sea, returning to their natal streams to spawn. Males develop a powerful kype, or hooked lower jaw, which is used as a weapon to defend spawning sites. Returning Atlantic Salmon do not eat once they return to fresh waters.

Where fish have been in fresh waters for a long time, products from the breakdown of stored food reserves accumulate in the skin and give it a red tinge.

Conservation: Atlantic Salmon are vulnerable to many threats during their complex life-cycle, including poor water quality, overfishing, excessive predation and obstructions to their passage up and down rivers. As salmon parr are territorial, populations are also limited by the availability of suitable habitat and adequate stretches of river are, therefore, a critical requirement. Atlantic Salmon are of direct conservation importance, scheduled for example under the Bern Convention and EU Habitats Directive. However, they also play important roles in the life-cycles of other species, including those of conservation concern. Perhaps the most remarkable relationship is with the Freshwater Pearl Mussel *Margaritifera margaritifera*, an Endangered mollusc found on the beds of just a few exceptionally clean English, Welsh and Scottish rivers. These mussels depend upon fish, including salmon parr and Brown Trout, as their glochidia larvae are released into the water column and attach to the gills of their fish host, where they grow and are dispersed as the fish moves during the coming winter, detaching in the spring to drop into clean, fine gravel where they begin independent adult lives.

Identifying salmon and trout parr

The parr of Atlantic Salmon and Brown/Sea Trout may both be found inhabiting shallow, gravel-bedded reaches of rivers where the two species breed. Although detailed identification of immature fishes is beyond the scope of this book, Atlantic Salmon parr can usually be distinguished from the parr of Brown/Sea Trout by their larger pectoral fins, smaller mouths and a range of other features, as highlighted below:

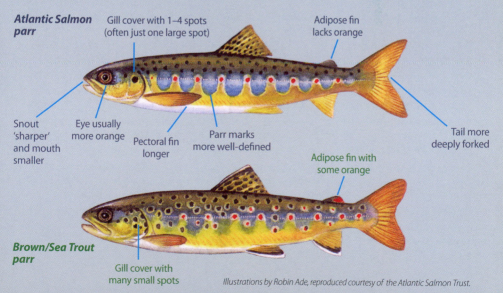

Atlantic Salmon parr

Gill cover with 1–4 spots (often just one large spot)

Adipose fin lacks orange

Snout 'sharper' and mouth smaller

Eye usually more orange

Pectoral fin longer

Parr marks more well-defined

Tail more deeply forked

Adipose fin with some orange

Brown/Sea Trout parr

Gill cover with many small spots

Illustrations by Robin Ade, reproduced courtesy of the Atlantic Salmon Trust.

Brown Trout or Sea Trout   *Salmo trutta*

Other names: The Brown Trout is known locally as 'Brownie'; Sea Trout is also known regionally as 'Sewen' (in Wales), 'Peel' (in south west England) 'Finnock' (in Scotland) and 'Salmon Trout' (in culinary circles).

Least Concern	
Native	
Common and widespread	
Riverine, Estuarine	
Max. length:	140 cm (55 inches)
Max. weight:	30 kg (66 lb)

The Brown Trout is so adaptable in form and lifestyle that it was formerly thought to have been many different species (see *page 130*). These include the Sea Trout, which has a similar life-cycle to the Atlantic Salmon (*page 80*), and the Ferox, which grows to a large size and develops fearsome jaws adapting it to a piscivorous diet in deep, cool lakes. The Brown or Sea Trout is a fish of clean and cool streams, rivers and lakes, with the Sea Trout also occupying estuaries and coastal seas. It is widespread off the north-western coast of Europe and southwards as far as the north-west coast of Asia, but has been widely introduced elsewhere in the world. Brown Trout are of considerable commercial value through recreational angling and aquaculture.

Identification: The Brown Trout shares the streamlined body form of the Atlantic Salmon, with similar numbers of fin rays (III–IV spines and 10–12 soft rays in the dorsal fin, and III–IV spines and 12–14 soft rays in the anal fin). It has a small head and a large mouth armed with short, strong teeth. Body colouration varies markedly depending on the habitat and life-cycle of the specific trout population, but is generally a grey-blue background colour with numerous spots that occur both above and below the lateral line. Many freshwater populations have the buttery-brownish background body colour that gives the Brown Trout its name, whilst sea-going fish take on a similar silver sheen to salmon.

Ecology: Brown Trout always breed in cool, well-oxygenated rivers with suitable spawning gravels. Freshwater resident stock generally matures at between three and four years, running up rivers or entering the tributary streams of lakes to breed. Males guard territories in which female fish cut one or

Brown Trout are readily distinguished from Rainbow Trout (*page 86*) by the lack of that species' pink or red stripe along the side, and also, generally, by a lack of spots on the tail.

Features that distinguish adult Sea Trout from Atlantic Salmon include:

- the extension of the mouth behind the eye
- the presence of spots on the body below the lateral line
- the lack of the salmon's pronounced 'wrist' before the tail fin.

Hybrids between Brown Trout and Atlantic Salmon often occur (estimated at around 7% of the British population) due to similar spawning habits; hybrid fish share intermediate features.

Trout parr differ from those of salmon by having fewer and less distinct dark 'parr marks' ('dirty fingerprints') along the sides, as well as shorter pectoral fins. They also tend to hang in midwater rather than closer to the river bed. **See *page 83* for more details.**

more redds in coarse gravel, laying as many as 10,000 eggs. These hatch in late winter or early spring. The parr feed mainly on aquatic and terrestrial insects as well as molluscs, crustaceans and small fish. Trout can be long-lived in some environments, particularly Ferox which can reach a maximum reported age of 38 years.

Although Sea Trout have a similar freshwater biology to salmon, their marine stage is different. They spend between one and five years in fresh water, depending on environmental conditions, and anything between six months and five years in coastal seas and estuaries.

Sea Trout (above) and Brown Trout (below) showing typical body shape and colour, although both may vary with habitat conditions and between locally adapted strains.

Rainbow Trout

Oncorhynchus mykiss

Other names: Rainbow, Blue Trout, Steelhead

The natural distribution of the Rainbow Trout is in rivers flowing into the Pacific along the west coast of North America from Alaska to Mexico, where a sea-going form, the Steelhead occurs. However, this species has been widely introduced across the temperate waters of the world as a source of food and for recreational angling; it is commonly produced for these purposes in aquaculture. In the British Isles, 'wild' fish are regularly encountered in rivers and large lakes with good water quality due to frequent introductions for angling purposes as well as releases from fish farms. However, only some populations are known to breed. Sea-going Steelhead populations have not become established in the UK. Rainbow Trout feed on aquatic and terrestrial invertebrates and small fishes, and can live for up to 11 years.

Identification: The streamlined body is elongate and somewhat laterally compressed. The dorsal and anal fins lack spines but are supported respectively by 10–12 and 8–12 soft rays, and the caudal (tail) fin has 19 rays. There is a characteristic wide pink to red stripe along the flank from the head to the caudal base, although this is lacking in the sea-running Steelhead and in the cultivated form known as 'Blue Trout'. Typically, spotting continues onto the tail, unlike in the Brown Trout (*page 84*).

Not evaluated	
Introduced, Naturalized	
ILFA Import restriction	
Locally common	
Riverine, Still Water	
Max. length:	120 cm (47 inches)
Max. weight:	25·4 kg (60 lb)

Ecology: Rainbow Trout generally undertake short spawning migrations into suitable streams with a clean gravel bottom, although this behaviour is rare in the British Isles. Spawning behaviour is typical of the salmonids (see *pages 10–11*).

Conservation: The predatory Rainbow Trout is a significant threat to a range of British wildlife, and adverse environmental impacts have also reported from several other countries. It feeds on species that may be of conservation concern, including amphibians, large invertebrates and small fishes, and also competes with native predatory fishes. In the UK, trade in, and the keeping of, Rainbow Trout is controlled under the Import of Live Fish (England and Wales) Act 1980. There is an increasing trend to stock with triploid Rainbow Trout (sterile fish with three sets of chromosomes) that not only grow faster, benefitting aquaculture and angling interests, but also require continual stocking in order to maintain populations.

The Rainbow Trout is a 'familiar alien' in British running and still fresh waters. Introduced widely for angling purposes as well as escaping from trout farms, it also breeds in some rivers.

Farmed fish released into the wild can generally be distinguished by their worn or deformed dorsal, tail and pectoral fins as a result of growing in confined space, as seen in the image above.

FACING PAGE: *A commercial trout farm, fed by water diverted from a chalk river and containing many trout fed with concentrated pellet feed.*

Grayling

Thymallus thymallus

Other names: Umber, 'Lady of the stream'

The Grayling has no migratory life-phase, unlike other salmonids, and inhabits running, well-oxygenated waters. It is a characteristic species of clear, upper reaches of rivers with sand, gravel or rocky beds and is extremely sensitive to pollution. The non-migratory nature of their life-cycle has meant that Grayling have never penetrated Irish waters. They have been introduced to many rivers in Scotland and south-west England. Grayling are gregarious, often found in small- to medium-sized shoals, feeding and remaining active even in cool conditions. The diet comprises mainly aquatic insects and their nymphs and larvae, small worms and crustaceans.

Identification: Due to their elongated, graceful appearance – streamlined with silvery, iridescent flanks dappled with irregular dark spots interspersed with hints of purple, green and copper, and with a characteristic prominent 'sail-like' dorsal fin – Grayling

Least Concern		
Bern Convention (App. III)		
Habitats Directive (Ann. V)		
Native		
Localized		
Riverine		
Max. length:		60 cm (24 inches)
Max. weight:		2·7 kg (6 lb 10 oz)

sometimes delight in the title of 'Lady of the stream'. The distinctive dorsal fin, mottled with black and red bars and raised at times of stress or to 'sail' in strong currents, also indicates the gender of the fish: males have the largest and deepest-hued fins, which they use for display at spawning time. The mouth is toothless and well adapted for feeding predominantly on the river bed, with the top lip extending beyond the lower. This may explain why Grayling

feeding at the surface tend to roll and splash as they intercept floating food items.

Another curious feature is the smell of Grayling when caught, which is often likened to fresh thyme, and from which the species derives its scientific name.

Ecology: Unlike other British salmonids, Grayling spawn in the spring, typically from March to June depending upon the local climate. At spawning time, the body colour of males darkens and intensifies, and the spectacular iridescent blue-red dorsal and pelvic fins are held erect to display to females and entice them to dig redds and lay their eggs. They are communal spawners, though males defend territories within a spawning group of fish and run to these territories on a daily basis rather than remaining there. Most spawning takes place as water temperatures peak in the early afternoon and tends to occur on suitable gravels close to the habitats in which they spend most of their lives. However, in colder regions Grayling may undertake spawning migrations up river following the spring thaw. Grayling mature at three or four years old, relatively fast for a fish of cooler climates, and their high fecundity means that populations can recover quickly from any dip in numbers.

Conservation: Since Grayling have some of the most exacting water quality requirements of any freshwater fish species, they are valuable indicators of pollution. The species is of direct conservation importance and is listed under the Bern Convention and also the EU Habitats Directive (see *page 133*). In the past, Grayling has been subject to a degree of persecution due to their perceived competition for food with more prized game fishes (salmon and trout), as well as their keenness to intercept an angler's fly intended for other salmonids. Today, though, this species is generally treated with more respect.

Arctic Charr

Salvelinus alpinus

Other names: Char, Torgoch (Wales), 'Tartan-fins'

Arctic Charr has the most northerly distribution of any freshwater fish species, being cold-tolerant and found in both fresh and salt water across a wide Arctic and sub-Arctic range. British Arctic Charr occur in the deeper waters of large, deep lakes, and are generally considered a glacial relict species. Their tolerance of cold conditions means that they are one of the main aquatic predators in the cool regions of the northern hemisphere. This is a schooling species, preying mainly on smaller fishes. Several charr fisheries were established in British waters going back to at least the mid-19th century and perhaps to medieval times, for example on Lake Windermere, but these fisheries have now ceased to be commercially important.

Identification: The Arctic Charr shares many of its characteristics with the closely

Least Concern		
Native		
UK BAP Priority Species (except Northern Ireland)		
Localized		
Glacial lakes		
Max. length:		107 cm (42 inches)
Max. weight:		15 kg (33 lb)

related Atlantic Salmon (*page 80*) and Brown/Sea Trout (*page 84*). This includes an elongated and streamlined body, oblong in profile and rounded in cross-section, and a small head and large mouth armed with teeth for a mobile, predatory lifestyle. The scales are very fine and also deeply embedded, giving the skin a smooth, slippery feel. However, unlike trout, Arctic Charr possess teeth only in the central forward part of the mouth. Other differences between species of charr and trout are less obvious, but include a distinctive boat-shaped bone in the upper part of the mouth of the charrs. Body colour varies dramatically with habitat and is so variable in fresh waters that, much as for the Brown Trout, different strains were once thought of as separate species – though there is a predominance of greens, reds and ambers (leading some anglers to call it by the nickname 'tartan-fins').

Ecology: Arctic Charr spawn in the well-oxygenated deeper gravel beds in lakes or in tributary rivers during autumn or winter, when water temperatures reach around 4°C. At this stage, these generally schooling fishes become territorial, with larger specimens, particularly mature males, defending optimal spawning gravels in which they coax female fish to cut depressions known as 'redds' and deposit their eggs, in much the same way as Atlantic Salmon and Brown Trout. Body colour intensifies as spawning approaches, and males tend to develop a kype on the lower jaw with which to defend spawning territories. Once the eggs have been released, the female covers them by fanning gravel back over the redd, often digging another redd in the process. This performance is repeated a number of times until she is spent. Juveniles grow slowly, reflecting the relatively low availability of food in cold water, though little is known of the early development of this deepwater species.

Conservation: The Arctic Charr is one of the rarest fish species in the British Isles, warranting particular conservation attention and their inclusion in the UK Biodiversity Action Plan. Populations are particularly vulnerable to elevated nutrient enrichment, which promotes blooms of algae that subsequently decompose, robbing oxygen from the cooler, deeper layers of water in which the fish shoal and feed. Acidification and the silting of spawning gravels also pose particular threats.

European Whitefish

Coregonus lavaretus

Other names: Powan (in Loch Lomond), Schelly or Skelly (in Haweswater, Ullswater and Red Tarn in the English Lake District), Gwyniad (in Llyn Tegid [Lake Bala] in Wales) and Pollan (in Northern Ireland)

The superficially herring-like European Whitefish is a cold water species inhabiting deeper regions of large lakes. Being somewhat more tolerant of warmer water than other whitefish species, it is the most widely distributed whitefish in western Europe and is the only whitefish to be found in shallow lakes.

In Wales, the population in Lake Bala is considered by some authorities, including the IUCN, which publishes the Red List (see *page 132*), to be a separate species – the Gwyniad *Coregonus pennantii*. The Scottish population, which is endemic to Loch Lomond and Loch Eck, is also considered by some authorities, again including the IUCN, to be a separate species – the Powan *Coregonus clupeoides*.

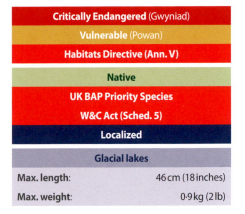

Critically Endangered (Gwyniad)	
Vulnerable (Powan)	
Habitats Directive (Ann. V)	
Native	
UK BAP Priority Species	
W&C Act (Sched. 5)	
Localized	
Glacial lakes	
Max. length:	46 cm (18 inches)
Max. weight:	0·9 kg (2 lb)

In Northern Ireland, the Pollan is sometimes treated as a separate species too (*Coregonus autumnalis*). However, the broader consensus is that the European Whitefish is one species, comprising scattered populations that have persisted since glacial times in deep, cold water lakes across northern Europe.

Identification: Although the European Whitefish varies in form throughout its range it typically has a laterally compressed, spindle-like body with a bluish or dark green, often very dark back. The head is conical and there are 35–39 fairly long and well-developed gill rakers. The maxillary bone reaches to the front of the eye or only just past it. The small, ventral mouth sometimes has minute teeth on either or both the jaws or tongue. The tips of the pectoral and pelvic fins are dusky, sometimes for up to half their length and the dorsal, anal and tail fins are dark. The dorsal, pectoral and pelvic fins are large and conspicuous compared to the closely related Vendace.

Ecology: Breeding from October to January, and exceptionally into March, European Whitefish spawn on marginal gravels around lake shorelines when the water is about 6°C. Adapted to cool waters, their growth rate is slow, with juvenile fish attaining just 6 cm (2·5") in their first year. However, individuals can live for up to ten years. The species feeds largely on benthic and planktonic invertebrates, with some populations known to rise up in the water column to feed by night.

Conservation: Like all whitefish, this species requires deep, good quality, well-oxygenated water. The principal threat is pollution, particularly by organic matter and nutrient enrichment, which robs the deeper water layers of oxygen. However, the Welsh population (the Gwyniad) is threatened not only by deteriorating water quality but also by

ENGLAND
1 Brotherswater
2 Haweswater
3 Red Tarn
4 Ullswater

SCOTLAND
5 Loch Eck
6 Loch Lomond

WALES
7 Llyn Tegid (Lake Bala)

NORTHERN IRELAND & EIRE
8 Lough Allen
9 Lough Derg
10 Lough Erne (Lower)
11 Lough Neagh
12 Lough Ree

The natural distribution of the European Whitefish in Britain and Ireland.

the introduction of Ruffe (*page 98*) to the lake in the 1980s. This species eats the vulnerable Gwyniad eggs and fry and, as a conservation measure, Gwyniad eggs have been transferred to Llyn Arenig Fawr, a nearby cold water lake.

Due to conservation concerns, the Scottish population (the Powan), has also been successfully translocated into two new sites: Loch Sloy and the Carron Valley Reservoir.

Gwyniad

Vendace

Coregonus albula

Other names: European Cisco

The Vendace, like other whitefish, superficially resembles a herring. In Britain, the species inhabits the deeper layers of a relatively small number of large, cold water lakes, although marine and estuarine populations occur around the Baltic Sea. Vendace form pelagic schools in deeper lakes and feed mainly on planktonic crustaceans.

Identification: The Vendace has an elongated but laterally compressed body, with a bluish or dark green, often very dark back. The head is conical and there are 34–52 long, well-developed gill rakers. The small, ventral mouth sometimes has minute teeth on either or both the jaws or tongue. The lower jaw fits in a narrow groove in the upper jaw and protrudes slightly beyond it. The dorsal, anal and tail fins have darker outer edges, and the tail is deeply forked.

Ecology: Due to the mainly deep water life-cycle of Vendace, relatively little is known about their ecology beyond their shoaling behaviour and their mainly invertebrate diet. However, Vendace may be seen from November to January when they move into shallower (3–10 m deep) water to spawn on sand or gravel substrates. There are spring-spawning populations of Vendace in several northern European lakes that some authorities consider to be a separate species. There is no brood care of the eggs once laid and fertilized.

Least Concern	
Habitats Directive (Ann. V)	
Native	
UK BAP Priority Species (England & Scotland only)	
W&C Act (Sched. 5)	
Localized	
Glacial lakes	
Max. length:	48 cm (19 inches)
Max. weight:	1 kg (2·2 lb)

In their cool water habitat the growth rate of juveniles is slow, although fish can live for up to ten years.

Conservation: Like all whitefish, the Vendace requires well-oxygenated, good quality water. Given their deep-water habitat in nutrient-poor lakes, pollution, particularly by organic matter and nutrient enrichment that collectively deplete oxygen from deeper water layers, poses a significant threat. Inputs of sediment into shallow spawning grounds has also been identified as a major conservation concern. The effects of these factors are further exacerbated by the introduction of coarse fish species, such as Roach (*page 55*) and Ruffe (*page 98*), which consume the eggs and fry of the Vendace and are implicated in its extinction from Bassenthwaite Lake in the English Lake District.

Pike family
Esocidae

1 British species
(native)

The family Esocidae comprises five species of predatory fishes, all within the single genus Esox, that inhabit the cooler, fresh waters of Eurasia and North America, although some species may enter brackish waters. They have duckbill-like snouts armed with strong teeth. The tail (caudal) fin is forked. The body is covered by small, circular scales. All species are predatory, feeding on a wide variety of fishes and other vertebrates, but only one occurs in Britain and Ireland.

Pike

Esox lucius

Other names: 'Freshwater Shark'

Pike are large, predatory freshwater fish that occur in standing and flowing waters and also the upper, more dilute reaches of estuaries. Their explosive acceleration, enabled by a long and powerful muscular body with anal and dorsal fins set well to the rear, and their big eyes and cavernous mouth mean the fish is well-equipped as an efficient 'ambush predator'. However, it may also seek out dead fish by smell. Pike prey predominantly upon other fish, and are cannibalistic, but will also take small amphibians, mammals and birds, including ducklings. Juveniles feed on small invertebrates but rapidly progress to a piscivorous diet. Pike have pronounced solitary habits and are usually found in the middle to lower layers of water, generally in association with submerged vegetation and other obstructions in which they lie in wait for prey.

Identification: The long, streamlined profile of the Pike and its large mouth armed with strong teeth, but lacking barbels, is unlikely to lead to confusion with any other British species of fish. The scales are small and the eyes are located on the upper part of the head, an adaptation for seeing prey passing above. The fins are soft-rayed and rounded, and the anal and dorsal fins are set well back on the body near the tail fin. The flanks are usually a mottled green colour, providing excellent camouflage, although the colouration is variable and adapted to local conditions.

Ecology: Pike spawn early in the year, from late February to May depending on the

Least Concern	
Native	
Common and widespread	
Riverine, Still Water, Estuarine	
Max. length:	130 cm (51 inches)
Max. weight:	27 kg (50 lb)

conditions. Large females move to vegetated backwaters or shallows, where they are accompanied by several, considerably smaller, competing males. Potential mates can end up being prey if the female is not receptive. The eggs are sticky and adhere to vegetation, juveniles emerging to exploit the bounty of other, later-spawning, species and also preying on their siblings. There is no parental care.

Conservation: In order to thrive, Pike require unpolluted water and a variety of aquatic habitats, where they can find ample food at all their life-stages, sufficient ambush sites and refuges from predators including larger Pike and otters. A diversity of marginal habitat is important for spawning and the survival of fry.

Owing to the Pike's pronounced cannibalistic tendencies, the removal of large individuals in over-managed fisheries can lead to an explosion in the number of smaller, fast-growing Pike. This may, in practice, be more damaging to the fishery than self-limitation of Pike numbers due to cannibalism.

Pike, the 'freshwater shark', is a streamlined ambush predator that occurs in fresh and dilute brackish waters throughout the British Isles.

Perch family
Percidae

3 British species
(2 native; 1 introduced)

The family Percidae comprises 159 species of largely freshwater fishes across the northern hemisphere, although some occur in estuaries. There are two dorsal fins, which may be separate or narrowly joined, the anterior is generally strongly spined.

Perch

Perca fluviatilis

Other names: European Perch

The Perch is a striking, boldy-marked predatory fish that is found in both standing and flowing waters, including the upper, more dilute reaches of estuaries. It is a shoaling species generally found in the middle to lower layers of the water column, often near sunken trees, submerged vegetation and other obstructions, from which they launch predatory raids. The young feed extensively on small invertebrates, whereas older individuals consume small fishes and large invertebrates. Shoals of hunting Perch are often the cause of 'explosions' of small prey fish at the surface as dusk approaches.

Identification: Perch possess two dorsal fins, the front one erected with strong spines and the rear one by soft rays. The conspicuous black spot on the membrane to the rear of the first spined dorsal fin is distinctive. There is also a clear gap between the two dorsal fins. They also have distinctive black, vertical stripes on their flanks over a generally greenish backdrop, and their small scales are rough to the touch. The lower fins tend to be a bright red. The mouth lacks barbels and the jaw lacks teeth, although the inner surface of the mouth is rough to aid the capture of prey.

Perch are not known to hybridize with other species.

Least Concern	
Native	
Common and widespread	
Riverine, Still Water	
Max. length:	60 cm (24 inches)
Max. weight:	2·7 kg (6 lb)

Small Perch may sometimes be confused with Ruffe (*page 98*), but are distinguished by the following features:

- The strong vertical bars on the side of the fish.
- There is a conspicuous and distinctive black spot on the membrane to the rear of the first, spined, dorsal fin.
- The two dorsal fins being separated (joined in Ruffe).

Ecology: Perch spawn in shoals on hard surfaces, with branches that dip into water margins being particularly favoured. They spawn between April and June depending on the conditions, and there is no parental care.

Conservation: In addition to good water quality, Perch require a range of aquatic habitats that support a diversity of prey items and opportunities for efficient hunting. Areas of deep water are particularly important for overwintering. Good habitat complexity enables the Perch to evade predators, such as cormorants and Pike, during all its life-stages, and also provides options for spawning. Stunted populations of Perch may be found in small stillwaters where their high fecundity results in food resources being outstripped.

The boldly-patterned Perch is a common shoaling predator found in fresh running and still waters throughout the British Isles.

Ruffe

Gymnocephalus cernua

Other names: Tommy Ruffe

Ruffe are found in standing and flowing waters across mainland Britain, although many populations beyond a native range in lowland England are a result of introductions. Despite their small size, they are primarily a predatory species. Young fish feed extensively on small invertebrates, while older fish consume mainly larger invertebrates, but will also take other small fish and fish eggs. The Ruffe is a shoaling species, generally encountered in the middle to lower layers of water, often near sunken trees, submerged vegetation and other obstructions that provide refuge.

Identification: The Ruffe has two joined dorsal fins, the front one held up by spines and the rear one by soft rays. It has small scales, generally silvery flanks (colouration varying according to conditions) and, normally, pale translucent fins. The mouth lacks barbels and although the jaw lacks teeth, the capture of prey is aided by the mouth's rough inner surface. Females are generally slightly larger than males and tend to live a little longer.

Ruffe are not known to hybridize.

Ecology: Ruffe gather in spawning shoals in shallow water from March to May depending on the conditions. Each female deposits between 1,000 and 6,000 eggs in sticky strands that adhere to vegetation and stones. There is no parental care. The growth rate is slow,

Least Concern	
Native	
Locally common	
Riverine, Still Water	
Max. length:	20 cm (8 inches)
Max. weight:	170 g (6 oz)

Ruffe may sometimes be confused with small Perch (*page 96*) but are distinguished by the following features:

- Ruffe lack the strong bar pattern on the flanks that characterize Perch.
- The two dorsal fins of the Ruffe are joined, whereas those of Perch are clearly separate.

both sexes maturing by their second year and reaching a maximum age of five to six years.

Conservation: In addition to good water quality, Ruffe require a complexity of aquatic habitats in order to thrive. Such conditions provide many options for spawning, enable them to find a good range of prey and ensures that there is plenty of cover to help them evade predators. Areas of deep water are important overwintering habitat. The introduction of Ruffe to some waters to which they are not native is a cause of concern for the conservation of other species, including Gwyniad (*page 91*) and Vendace (*page 93*), the eggs and fry of which are predated by Ruffe.

Zander

Sander lucioperca

Other names: Pike-perch

The Zander is a distinct species and not a hybrid of Pike (*page 94*) and Perch (*page 96*), as is commonly thought – as also suggested by its alternative common name. Zander were introduced to Britain from mainland Europe, where they are widespread, and have now spread throughout the Ouse, Thames and Severn river systems. They are found in both standing and flowing waters where there is adequate depth, favouring the middle to lower layers. The Zander is a largely crepuscular or nocturnal predator that feeds mainly on other fish, sometimes hunting as a pack. Juveniles feed extensively on small invertebrates.

Another species of 'pike-perch', the Walleye *Sander vitreus* from the Americas, was introduced into British waters at the start of the 20th century but failed to establish.

Identification: Like other members of the perch family, Zander possess two dorsal fins, the front one held up by spines and the rear one by soft rays; there is a distinct gap between these fins. The flanks are generally silver with a greenish tinge, although the colouration varies with local conditions. The scales are small, the

Least Concern	
Introduced, Naturalized	
W&C Act (Sched. 9)	
ILFA Import restriction	
Locally common	
Riverine, Still Water	
Max. length:	100 cm (39 inches)
Max. weight:	9 kg (20 lb)

The Zander is distinguished from Pike (*page 94*) and Perch (*page 96*) by a combination of the following features:

- The presence of two dorsal fins.
- The elongated body and the presence of teeth along the jaw.

fins are generally pale and translucent, and the eyes are distinctively large and reflective, giving a 'dead eye' appearance (but well-adapted to feeding in very low light). The jaws are armed with teeth but lack barbels, and the inner surface of the mouth is also rough to aid the capture of prey.

Zander are not known to hybridize.

Ecology: Zander spawn between April and June, when the water temperature exceeds 12°C, in a range of submerged hard substrates including rocky shores, plant stems and the exposed roots of bankside trees. Each female produces between 200,000 to 500,000 eggs. Males keep the spawning substrate clean, and guard the eggs and newly hatched fry. Juveniles feed on zooplankton and other invertebrates, but resort to a predominantly piscivorous diet by the end of their first year. Zander mature at the age of 3–5 years.

Conservation: As an introduced predator, the Zander is perceived to be a potential problem in British freshwater ecosystems but is also welcomed as a sporting fish. It requires good water quality, although can thrive in turbid waters using its keen eyesight and adopting ambush hunting tactics. Varied habitat also provides Zander with diverse food items and ambush points, as well as enabling the Zander themselves to evade predators. Deep areas are important for overwintering and are used throughout the year.

Sheatfish catfish family
Siluridae

1 British species (introduced)

The family Siluridae comprises 100 species of freshwater fishes found across Europe and Asia, although some may enter brackish water. Some species can grow very large, including the Wels Catfish, which is the only member of the family to have become established in the British Isles.

Wels Catfish

Siluris glanis

Other names: Catfish

Although native to Asia and continental Europe, where it occurs in fresh and brackish waters, the Wels Catfish is not a native species in the British Isles. There have been many introductions to rivers and lakes, apparently due to angling interests, as individuals can grow very large. Wels Catfish are also known to be present in some larger British rivers. This is an active and voracious predator, engulfing other fish, waterfowl and mammals in its cavernous mouth.

Least Concern
Bern Convention (App. III)
Introduced, Naturalized
W&C Act (Sched. 9)
ILFA Import restriction
Localized
Still Water

Max. length:	500 cm (197 inches)
Max. weight:	306 kg (675 lb)

Identification: Although variable, the body and fin colour is generally a dark, mottled grey, but paler beneath. The body tapers gradually to the rear, not unlike an enormous tadpole. These fishes have large mouths, with three pairs of long barbels or 'whiskers'. The eyes are very small and widely spaced, positioned on the side of the broad head. The dorsal fin, which is small, lacks spines but is supported by

Wels Catfish are unlikely to be confused with any native species of fish in Britain, or indeed the fishes of Ireland, although the species is not currently known to occur there. Although smaller Wels Catfish could, conceivably, be mistaken for the introduced Black Bullhead (see *page 102*), there is a dramatic maximum size difference, the Wels Catfish being much larger, and having only three pairs of barbels, whereas the Black Bullhead has four.

3–5 soft rays. However, the anal fin is very long and supported by 84–92 rays.

Wels Catfish are not known to hybridize.

Ecology: The Wels Catfish is a nocturnal predator, usually inert and dormant during the day, when it can be found sheltering in cover, such as under submerged trees or in underwater caves. It breeds from mid-May to mid-July in marshy zones on the edge of lakes and large rivers, laying eggs on mounds of leaf-litter that are guarded by the male. The young are pigmented but otherwise appear similar to tadpoles, growing rapidly and feeding on a variety of invertebrates, reaching 30 cm (12") in their first year. As these fish grow, they progress to a wholly carnivorous diet. Wels Catfish require deep water if they are to overwinter successfully.

Conservation: Although not widespread, where it does occur the predatory Wels Catfish is a threat to other species of fish and to many groups of animals, some of which are of conservation concern. There are no management measures in place to control existing populations of Wels Catfish, although their introduction to new waters is prohibited.

North American freshwater catfish family
Ictaluridae

1 British species (introduced)

The Ictaluridae family comprises 45 species distributed from southern Canada to Guatemala. One species, the Black Bullhead, has become established in Continental Europe, including in the British Isles, although there is no evidence that it is breeding in British waters.

Black Bullhead

Ameiurus melas formerly *Ictalurus melas*

Other names: None

The Black Bullhead is not related to our native Bullhead (*page 106*) but is, instead, a small species of North American freshwater catfish. Although individuals can live for up to ten years and grow to 66 cm (26"), they are usually much smaller in European waters. This fish has a wide introduced range across Europe, and can form dense populations.

Identification: The Black Bullhead has eight barbels: two on the snout; two maxillary and four on the chin. The body is scaleless and there are three long, sharp spines that arm the fish, one on each of the leading rays of the pectoral and dorsal fins, which can inflict a painful stab that often becomes infected.

The Black Bullhead is not known to hybridize.

Ecology: The Black Bullhead is omnivorous and voracious, potentially competing with other species for food and also eating their spawn and juveniles.

Not evaluated	
Introduced, Non-breeding	
ILFA Import restriction	
Localized	
Still Water	
Max. length:	66 cm (26 inches)
Max. weight:	3·6 g (7 lb 11 oz)

Conservation: The Import of Live Fish (England and Wales) Act 1980 recognised the potential for this species to form self-sustaining populations in the fresh waters of the British Isles, as it has done across Continental Europe, and closed the door on new imports of this species to the UK. It is important to continue to monitor fresh waters for the presence of the Black Bullhead, and any evidence of it breeding, and to initiate control measures to ensure that it does not spread, to the detriment of native ecosystems.

Sunfish family
Centrarchidae

1 British species (introduced)

The family Centrarchidae comprises 27 species of fishes from the fresh waters of North America. The front and rear dorsal fins may be joined or separate, the front fin supported by strong spines. Most sunfish build nests, and some are valued as sport fish or as experimental subjects.

Pumpkinseed Sunfish

Lepomis gibbosus

Other names: Pumpkinseed, Pond Perch, Sunny

The Pumpkinseed Sunfish is native to North America and was introduced to mainland Europe and the British Isles in the 1890s as a desirable aquarium fish. Due to its hardy nature it has also been used in biological research, particularly for toxicological studies. Although originally only found in the wild in south-east England, it is now widespread in Britain, with populations from Somerset to as far north as County Durham.

Not evaluated	
Introduced, Naturalized	
W&C Act (Sched. 9)	
Prohibition Order	
Localized	
Still Water	
Max. length:	20 cm (8 inches)
Max. weight:	180 g (6 oz)

Identification: The Pumpkinseed Sunfish is a small, high-backed and laterally compressed fish with bright electric-blue highlights across the flanks and strong blue, green and red colouration around the head. The body profile gives these fishes their common name 'pumpkinseed'. The dorsal fin is long, comprising a spined front fin fused into a soft-rayed rear fin.

Ecology: The Pumpkinseed Sunfish naturally favours quiet, vegetated lakes and ponds, and pools alongside streams and small rivers. Its high fecundity and wide diet means that dense populations can become established quickly in ideal conditions. It has a broad predatory diet that includes invertebrates and small fishes as well as fish eggs.

Conservation: The spread, import and keeping of the Pumpkinseed Sunfish in British waters is controlled under the Wildlife and Countryside Act 1981 and also the Prohibition of Keeping or Release of Live Fish (Specified Species) Order 1998.

River Loach (or Hillstream Loach) family
Balitoridae

1 British species (native)

The Balitoridae is a Eurasian family of about 500 species of fishes that possess elongated bodies with inferior (downward-pointing) mouths surrounded by at least three pairs of barbels. The pelvic (ventral) fins are either separate or fused underneath the belly. These are largely river fishes, some of which are popular in the aquarium trade.

Stone Loach

Barbatula barbatula

Other names: Loach, Stoney, Beardie, Groundling

The Stone Loach is a secretive fish of running waters and, occasionally, the shorelines of lakes. It is generally nocturnal and conceals itself under stones and dead wood on sandy, muddy or stony bottoms, feeding mainly on invertebrates such as insect larvae, crustaceans and worms. Although it is largely solitary, favourable stones may harbour other loaches as well as Bullheads (*page 106*) and (in winter) Minnows (*page 74*). Although Stone Loach can grow to a length of 12 cm (5"), they are usually only around 7–6 cm (3") in length. Individuals can live for up to seven years.

Identification: The Stone Loach is an elongated, scaleless fish, rounded in cross-section at the front but tapering to a moderately laterally compressed cross-section towards the rear of the body. There are six barbels around the mouth, four (two pairs) of which are under the tip of the snout, with a further pair at the corners of the mouth. The lateral line is well developed towards

Least Concern
Native
Common and widespread
Riverine

Max. length:	12 cm (5 inches)
Max. weight:	20 g (1 oz)

Stone Loach may sometimes be confused with Spined Loach but lack the backward-pointing spines beneath the eyes that characterize that species, and have longer barbels. Although superficially similar to Gudgeon (*page 73*), Stone Loach are scaleless, have more numerous, long barbels, and tend to hide under cover.

the front of the fish. The skin colour varies markedly with habitat, but is usually a dull yellow-brown with irregular dark-brown patches fading to whitish or creamy-yellow on the belly. The fins are rounded and the dorsal fin is set well back on the body, originating slightly in front of the base of the pelvic fins. Stone Loach are not known to hybridize.

Ecology: Spawning takes place between April and June, female Stone Loach shedding their sticky eggs in several clusters amongst gravel, stones and weed. Sometimes, females may guard clumps of eggs. Faster-growing Stone Loach may mature after their first year, but most reach maturity at 2–3 years old.

Conservation: Stone Loach require good water quality and well-oxygenated conditions, including adequate flows, and are known to be sensitive to pollution. Well-flushed marginal gravel runs aid successful spawning and a diversity of aquatic habitats provides a variety of food sources and places in which to evade their numerous predators. It is also important that large stones or woody debris are available under which Stone Loach hide by day. Siltation of rivers is a particular problem as it can blind the hollows in which Stone Loach would normally find refuge.

Loach family
Cobitidae

1 British species (native)

The Cobitidae family, which has many similarities with the river loach (or hillstream loach) family (Balitoridae), comprises 100 species of fishes with a spindle- or worm-like body form inhabiting fresh waters across Eurasia and into Morocco. They are bottom-dwelling with a small, inferior (downward-pointing) mouth surrounded by three to six pairs of barbels. Members of this family possess a characteristic erectile spine beneath the eye. The Cobitidae include some popular aquarium fishes.

Spined Loach

Cobitis elongatoides

Other names: Loach, Spiney, Groundling

The Spined Loach is arguably one of our rarest native fishes being almost entirely restricted to the catchments of the rivers Trent, Great Ouse, Welland, Nene and Witham in eastern England. Spined Loach are secretive fish, favouring dense submerged vegetation in which to hide by day and emerging at night to feed on small bottom-living animals as well as vegetable matter. It is also one of Britain's smallest fishes, reaching 11·5 cm (4·5") (rarely 13·5 cm (5·5")) in length, when mature.

Least Concern	
Bern Convention (App. III)	
Habitats Directive (Ann. II)	
Native	
UK BAP Priority Species (England only)	
Localized	
Riverine	
Max. length:	13·5 cm (5·5 inches)
Max. weight:	30 g (1 oz)

Identification: The head and body of the Spined Loach are strongly compressed laterally, and the scales are minute. It is generally light brown in colour, with the sides straw-coloured and the belly yellow. Ten to nineteen brown spots run along the flanks from the head to the tail. The head is small and there are three pairs of short barbels around the small mouth. Below and just in front of each eye is a strong, movable double-pointed spine that points backwards and is often retracted into a skin fold. This is diagnostic. These characteristic spines, in addition to the shorter barbels, distinguish larger Spined Loach from small Stone Loach (*page 104*).

Ecology: Spined Loach spawn from April to June, depositing eggs on stones, plants or submerged roots. The eggs are not guarded. The small size of the fry and the adults means that dense vegetation and good

> Spined Loach may sometimes be confused with Stone Loach (*page 104*) but are distinguished by backward-pointing spines beneath the eyes, and they also possess shorter barbels. There are also superficial similarities with Gudgeon (*page 73*), though Spined Loach are minutely scaled, have more numerous, relatively long barbels, and tend to hide in vegetation.

habitat diversity are essential for successful reproduction. Such areas also provide important cover from predators and feeding opportunities.

Conservation: Spined Loach does not appear to have exacting water quality requirements. However, as dense vegetation is an essential habitat component, this species is especially vulnerable to insensitive weed cutting and dredging.

Sculpin family
Cottidae

1 British species (native)

The family Cottidae comprises 300 freshwater, brackish and marine species found across the northern hemisphere and near New Zealand. The body often appears scaleless, although scales or prickles are also commonly found. The eyes are set high on the head. These are bottom-dwelling fishes, lacking a swim bladder, at least in adult fish. Members of the Cottidae family guard their eggs.

Bullhead
Cottus gobio

Other names: Miller's Thumb, Bullyhead, Mullyhead

The Bullhead is a small species found in gravel and rocky reaches of flowing waters and the turbulent edges of larger still waters from the North Baltic southwards across Europe to Mediterranean drainage basins. Bullheads lack a swim bladder and inhabit the bed of flowing waters. They are solitary, making territories beneath large stones that they may defend and inhabit for all of their lives. This is an exclusively carnivorous species, feeding on invertebrates and fish fry.

Identification: The Bullhead is large-headed with a big mouth and a pair of small eyes on

Least Concern		
Habitats Directive (Ann. II)		
Native		
Common and widespread		
Riverine		
Max. length:		10 cm (4 inches)
Max. weight:		20 g (0·7 oz)

the top of its head. The mottled brown body tapers away behind the head. Although the body is covered in scales, these are small and the skin soft, giving a scaleless appearance. Bullheads possess two dorsal fins, the front one shorter and spined and the rearmost held up with soft rays. The anal fin is long, and the pectoral fins are large. The fins are mottled, matching the pattern of the body, but are paler.

Bullheads share a similar habitat to the Stone Loach (*page 104*), but are not easily confused with other species of fishes.

Ecology: During the spawning season, from March to May depending on local conditions, male Bullheads entice neighbouring females into excavations under their territorial stones. The female deposits around 100 sticky eggs in clusters on the underside of the stone, the male fertilizing them before driving the female off. The male Bullhead then nurtures the eggs through to hatching and cares for the fry until they are free-swimming, after which they disperse to find cover and ultimately establish their own territories.

Conservation: Bullheads require high water quality and a good flow of oxygenated water, being found most frequently in riffles where fast water runs over large stones. This gravel or rocky substrate provides diverse invertebrate and small fish food items, as well as providing refuge from predators such as other fishes (e.g. Perch, small Pike, trout and Chub) or piscivorous birds (e.g. kingfishers and grebes). Siltation is a particular threat to the Bullhead, as it 'blinds' the habitat beneath stones under which they live.

Bullheads frequent clean, fresh water in rivers, streams and the margins of larger stillwaters, forming solitary territories under stones which they may inhabitat throughout their entire life.

Sturgeon family
Acipenseridae

**1 British species
(native; predominantly marine
but spawns in freshwater rivers)**

The 23 species within the family Acipenseridae are large fishes of cold to temperate fresh, brackish and marine waters in the Northern Hemisphere. They are anadromous, inhabiting marine waters and breeding in running fresh waters. The body is elongated and has five rows of large armoured scales (scutes) along the sides. The mouth is small, inferior (beneath the snout), toothless and protractile, with four barbels in front. The swim bladder is large. Historically, sturgeons have been important for their meat and their roe (caviar), although nearly all species are now globally threatened.

Common Sturgeon

Acipenser sturio

Other names: European Sturgeon

The Common Sturgeon is an anadromous species, living out its adult life at sea and returning to fresh waters to spawn, where it inhabits deeper water and stays close to the bed. This very large fish can live for up to 100 years. It is a very scarce and solitary visitor to British waters, occasionally found entering lower estuaries from the sea. Its name belies the fact that this fish is anything but 'common'; although there is evidence that it occurred more frequently in previous centuries, it is now thought to be on the verge of extinction.

Identification: A large, elongated fish with five distinctive rows of scutes (large bony scales) along the body that serve as a defence

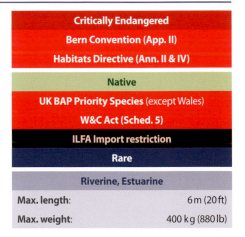

Critically Endangered	
Bern Convention (App. II)	
Habitats Directive (Ann. II & IV)	
Native	
UK BAP Priority Species (except Wales)	
W&C Act (Sched. 5)	
ILFA Import restriction	
Rare	
Riverine, Estuarine	
Max. length:	6 m (20 ft)
Max. weight:	400 kg (880 lb)

against predators. The back is olive-blue fading to paler on the underside. The mouth is small and inferior beneath an elongated and pointed snout, and is toothless and protractile, enabling the fish to extract invertebrate and fish prey from sediments. There are four barbels midway between the tip of the snout and the mouth, which are diagnostic. These features, combined with the characteristic elongated body, should be sufficient to distinguish the Common Sturgeon from other fishes found in British lower rivers and estuaries.

All species of sturgeon stray far and wide during their seagoing adult life, so it is possible that other species may enter British estuaries and lower rivers.. However, since these species are also very rare, the chances of such an occurrence are considered to be negligible. The Common Sturgeon is not known to hybridize.

Ecology: Little is known about the marine habits of any species of migratory sturgeon, but mature fish enter rivers to breed. Details of the breeding habits of the Common Sturgeon are also poorly understood, but the eggs are deposited on sand, gravel and stones, with juveniles subsequently being found both in estuaries and in the open sea. This slow-growing, long-lived species matures at 7–9 years of age, female fish releasing 800,000–2,400,000 dark, sticky eggs at each spawning.

Conservation: The major threats to all species of sturgeon are by-catch in fisheries for other species, estuarine pollution, degradation of spawning habitat, and obstructions to their free passage up rivers to spawn. Across their global range, the sturgeons have also suffered from poaching, primarily for the harvesting of caviar to support a lucrative market. The Common Sturgeon is now largely restricted to the Garonne drainage basin in France.

Hake and burbot family
Lotidae

1 British species (native but now considered extinct in Britain)

The cod-like family Lotidae comprises 21 mainly marine fishes. They possess between one and three dorsal fins, a single anal fin and a chin barbel, and the caudal (tail) fin is rounded. The Burbot is the only freshwater member of the family, and occurs in the northern parts of Eurasia and North America.

Burbot
Lota lota

Other names: Mariah, 'The Lawyer', Eelpout

The Burbot is the only member of its family, which is part of the Order Gadiformes or 'cod-like fishes', to be found in fresh water. Although it has a wide distribution in lakes and slow-flowing waters across the northern part of North America and Eurasia, it is now considered Extinct in the British Isles. However, rumours of its continued existence persist and the fish is included in the UK Biodiversity Action Plan. Burbots are adapted to cold waters, move slowly and are nocturnal in habit; they can live for up to 20 years.

Least Concern	
Native, now considered extinct	
UK BAP Priority Species	
ILFA Import restriction	
Extinct in the UK	
Riverine, Still Water	
Max. length:	152 cm (60 inches)
Max. weight:	34 kg (75 lb)

Identification: The Burbot's unusual 'cod-like' appearance is distinctive. It has an elongated, mottled body with two dorsal fins, the second of which is very long (lacking spines but supported by 67–96 soft rays), a rounded tail, long anal fin (with 58–79 soft rays but no spines) and a single barbel beneath the chin.

Burbot are not easy to confuse with other species of fish, and are not known to hybridize.

Ecology: Across their holarctic range, Burbot spawn in the winter, often under ice and as early as December through to mid-April. Mature individuals migrate into shallower waters of less than 3 m (10 ft) depth, males arriving first for spawning. Favoured spawning habitat is sand or gravel beds near the shore |or on mid-channel shoals.

Spawning is communal and nocturnal, with a s many as a dozen fish clustering into tight balls, the females shedding tiny eggs each containing an oil globule. The eggs float off into the water column, and there is no parental care. Burbot are hugely prolific, a large female releasing as many as one to three million eggs in a single spawning. The eggs come to rest on the lake or river bed and may get caught in the voids in gravel, where they lie for between 30 and 71 days before hatching. Larval Burbot migrate towards the surface as part of the plankton, feeding initially on the spring bloom of small planktonic animals and moving progressively to feed on larger invertebrates. As they grow, they migrate to deeper lakes and into bigger and deeper rivers to live out their adult lives, feeding predominantly on fish. Burbot grow slowly, an adaptation to cool waters, maturing after between two and seven years.

Conservation: Burbot require deep and cool slow-flowing rivers or large still waters that are of good water quality, as well as suitable sand or gravel marginal habitat on which to spawn in winter. Their main threats appear to be nutrient enrichment and habitat modification, which reduce oxygen concentrations and impact on their spawning and nursery grounds. Over-management of rivers to enhance the drainage function, including the removal of backwaters and slow-flowing marginal areas, also compromises the recruitment of fry. However, as the Burbot is officially Extinct in the British Isles, with little prospect of being reintroduced, such concerns are currently academic.

Herring, shad, sardine and menhaden family
Clupeidae

**2 British species
(both native marine species
that spawn in freshwater rivers)**

The family Clupeidae has a global, mainly tropical distribution in fresh, brackish and marine waters from latitudes of 70°N to about 60°S. The 216 species are mostly marine and coastal schooling fishes, with some freshwater and anadromous (running rivers from the sea to spawn) species. The body is usually spindle-shaped, rounded or strongly laterally compressed and generally herring-like. The head lacks scales, but the body usually has large, round and smooth scales. The teeth along the jaws are small or minute. The clupeids are one of the most important families of fish harvested for the commercial production of food, oil or fish meal.

Allis Shad
Alosa alosa

Other names: None

The Allis Shad is an increasingly uncommon species of British waters, although it is not of particular conservation concern across its broad natural range in the eastern Atlantic from Norway southwards to northern Mauritania (Africa). This is a schooling species, living at sea but running rivers in May or June to spawn. The maximum recorded age is ten years. It feeds on planktonic crustaceans, larger individuals also hunting small fishes. The adult fish are said not to feed when in fresh waters, but this seems to be untrue as, like Twaite Shad (*page 112*), they are readily taken by fly fishermen.

Identification: The Allis Shad is readily confused with Twaite Shad. The herring-like body of the Allis Shad is somewhat laterally compressed and also moderately deep, though body depth at the pectoral fin is less than the length of the head. The flanks are covered by large, thin scales. There is a dark spot immediately behind the gill opening but, unlike Twaite Shad, this is not followed by 7 or 8 similar spots along the flank. The upper jaw is notched, with a corresponding spike on the lower jaw fitting into it. The gill rakers, which are long (nearly or as long as the gill filaments), thin and numerous, are an important diagnostic feature. Allis Shad are not known to hybridize.

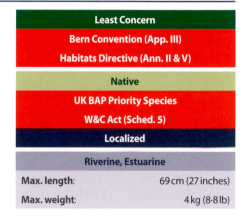

Least Concern		
Bern Convention (App. III)		
Habitats Directive (Ann. II & V)		
Native		
UK BAP Priority Species		
W&C Act (Sched. 5)		
Localized		
Riverine, Estuarine		
Max. length:		69 cm (27 inches)
Max. weight:		4 kg (8·8 lb)

Ecology: The migratory habit of the Allis Shad is related to its need to spawn in fresh running waters over gravel bottoms. Adults congregate near estuaries from February, entering rivers usually in May. The temperature at which they spawn is recorded as 22–24°C, far higher than that for Twaite Shad, though this is contradicted somewhat by the precise conditions in the few British rivers in which they spawn. These fish spawn near the surface over sand or gravel in large shoals by night and return to the sea shortly after spawning. Fry move down-river as they develop, most moving to the river mouth during their first summer. Juvenile Allis Shad remain close to shore and estuaries, males undertaking spawning runs upriver from 2–3 years old and females at 3–4 years.

Conservation: Although the Allis Shad is becoming increasingly scarce in British waters, it is of low conservation concern across its geographical range.

Pollution and impoundments or other obstructions to their free passage up and down river systems pose the major threats.

Twaite Shad   *Alosa fallax*

Other names: Twaite

The Twaite Shad, of which there are five known subspecies across its broad range from the coasts of southern Scandinavia southwards to Morocco, is an increasingly uncommon species of British waters. It is a schooling species, adults living at sea but running rivers in May or June to spawn. These are long-lived fish, with a maximum recorded age of 25 years. Twaite Shad feed on small fishes and crustaceans, prey size matching the size of its life-stage. In common with the Allis Shad (*page 111*), adult Twaite Shad are said not to feed when in fresh waters, although they are readily taken by fly fishermen during their spawning runs up rivers.

Least Concern		
Bern Convention (App. III)		
Habitats Directive (Ann. II & V)		
Native		
UK BAP Priority Species		
W&C Act (Sched. 5)		
Localized		
Riverine, Estuarine		
Max. length:		60 cm (24 inches)
Max. weight:		1·5 kg (3·3 lb)

Identification: Twaite Shad is very similar to Allis Shad and the two species are easy to confuse. The body of the Twaite Shad is herring-like, somewhat laterally compressed, although moderately deep, and covered by large, thin scales. The body depth at the pectoral fin is less than the length of the head. A dark spot is found immediately behind the gill opening, generally followed by 7 or 8 similar spots along the flank although these are sometimes faint or absent. The upper jaw is distinctly notched at its centre, the lower jaw being of equal length or fitting within the upper jaw. The gill rakers are an important diagnostic feature that help to distinguish Twaite Shad from the closely related Allis Shad, being not only fewer in number in the Twaite Shad but also shorter (less than the length of the gill filaments and often only a little more than half as long).

Twaite Shad are not known to hybridize.

Ecology: Mature Twaite Shad congregate near estuaries in April, entering rivers in May or early June when temperatures reach 10–12°C. They run river systems, locating upper reaches with clean gravel bottoms on which they spawn communally at night as a compact shoal. Twaite Shad may remain in the river for around two weeks, dropping back to sea shortly after spawning. As the fry develop, they progressively move down the river and reach the river mouth during their first summer. Juvenile Twaite Shad tend to remain close to shore or around estuaries, mainly feeding on plankton. The shad mature slowly, males undertaking spawning runs upriver from 2–3 years old and female fish from 3–4 years.

Conservation: Although the Twaite Shad is not of conservation concern across its wider geographical range, it is becoming increasingly scarce in British waters. This appears to be due to a combination of impoundments or other obstructions to free passage in river systems as well as various forms of pollution, although factors at sea also pose threats to the species.

Differentiating features of Allis Shad and Twaite Shad

Feature	Allis Shad	Twaite Shad
Dark spots on the flank behind the large spot to the rear of the gill cover	**Absent**	**Usually 7–8**
Spines and soft rays on the dorsal fin	IV–VI/13–**18**	IV–VI/**12**–16
Spines and soft rays on the anal fin	III–IV/16–22	III–IV/16–22
Gill rakers	**80–130**	**40–60**

Allis Shad

The Allis Shad (above) and Twaite Shad (below) are increasingly scarce species that live out their adult lives at sea but run a number of clean rivers to spawn in fresh waters in the late spring.

Twaite Shad

Stickleback and tubesnout family
Gasterosteidae

2 British species (both native)

The seven species within the family Gasterosteidae are small fishes found in fresh, brackish and marine waters of the northern hemisphere. Their bodies are generally elongated and either lack scales or are covered by scutes (large bony scales) along the sides. The mouth is usually small, located at the end of a narrow, tapering snout, and there are no barbels. Characteristically, between three to sixteen well-developed dorsal spines are found in front of a dorsal fin supported by soft rays.

Three-spined Stickleback

Gasterosteus aculeatus

Other names: 'Prickleback', Stickybag

The Three-spined Stickleback is a small though extremely hardy species of still waters, small streams, river edges, ditches and estuaries. It is commonly found in the margins of water bodies, sometimes forming dense shoals. In some rivers, particularly in Scotland, Three-spined Sticklebacks sometimes migrate downstream into estuaries and coastal waters to overwinter. This is primarily a carnivorous species that feeds on small invertebrates.

Least Concern	
Native	
Common and widespread	
Riverine, Still Water, Estuarine	
Max. length:	11 cm (4 inches)
Max. weight:	20 g (0·7 oz)

Although the Three-spined Stickleback may initially be confused with Ten-spined Stickleback (*page 116*), counting the spines that comprise the first dorsal fin is a foolproof way of separating the two species.

Identification: Three-spined Sticklebacks are streamlined and laterally compressed, and have body armour – a few large scales known as 'scutes' that provide a tough outer layer. The skin colour varies throughout the year (see below) but the fins are colourless. The first dorsal fin is reduced to the three prominent spines that give the species its common name, a smaller, soft-rayed dorsal fin being located behind them. The mouth is small and lacks barbels, and the eyes are large.

Ecology: In the spawning season, between April and June depending on local conditions, male Three-spined Sticklebacks develop a bright spawning livery of green or blue flanks and a brilliant red belly. They establish territories in which they build nests of vegetation glued together with secretions from their kidneys. To these they attract the silvery-coloured females using a characteristic 'zig-zag' dance. The females are driven off once they have laid their eggs. Male Three-spined Sticklebacks are devoted parents, fanning fresh water over the eggs and removing those that die, and they also defend the fry for the first few days after they become free-swimming.

Conservation: Three-spined Sticklebacks do not require high water quality, and can thrive even in stagnant or polluted water where competitors and predators struggle to survive. They frequent the margins and shallow areas of these waters, where they can find a diversity of food items and refuges from spates and predators.

Male Three-spined Sticklebacks (above) take on gaudy breeding colouration, including a characteristic red belly in the spring, whilst female fish (below) retain their more muted body colour.

Ten-spined Stickleback

Pungitius pungitius

Other names: Nine-spined Stickleback

The Ten-spined Stickleback is a small fish of still waters, small streams and river edges, where it favours dense vegetation and occasionally forms shoals. Owing to its preference for well-vegetated farm ponds, canals, streams and creeks, as well as being intolerant of strongly saline water, the distribution of the Ten-spined Stickleback is somewhat more restricted than that of the Three-spined Stickleback. Ten-spined Sticklebacks are primarily carnivorous, feeding on small invertebrates.

Least Concern	
Native	
Locally common	
Riverine, Still Water	
Max. length:	11 cm (4 inches)
Max. weight:	20 g (0·7 oz)

The Ten-spined Stickleback may be confused with the Three-spined Sticklebacks at first sight, but the 9–10 spines comprising the first dorsal fin is diagnostic.

Identification: Ten-spined Sticklebacks are more streamlined than Three-spined Sticklebacks (*page 114*), and of a more uniform buff or silvery colour throughout the year. The first dorsal fin, which is reduced to nine or ten spines (hence its common names), is less robust than that of the Three-spined Stickleback. A smaller, soft-rayed dorsal fin is located behind these spines. The body is slightly laterally compressed, the mouth is small and lacks barbels, the eyes are large, and the fins are colourless. This species is not known to hybridize.

Ecology: During the spawning season, usually April–June, male Ten-spined Sticklebacks become brighter, though not as gaudy as male Three-spined. They establish territories in which they build nests of vegetation glued together with secretions from their kidneys. The silvery-coloured females are attracted by a distinctive 'zig-zag' dance but are driven off once they have laid their eggs. The males tend the eggs, fanning fresh water over them and removing any that die. They also defend the fry for the first few days after they become free-swimming.

Conservation: Although the Ten-spined Stickleback does not require high water quality, it prospers less well than the Three-spined in polluted water. The habitat requirements of this fish are also more exacting than those of the Three-spined. It particularly favours densely vegetated margins and shallow areas that provide refuge and a variety of food items.

Freshwater eel family
Anguillidae

1 British species
(native; breeds at sea and migrates
to coastal and fresh waters)

The family Anguillidae comprises 15 species of long-bodied freshwater, marine and brackish water fishes in both tropical and temperate regions. The snake-like body is covered in minute scales, appearing scaleless, and is coated in thick slime, making eels slippery and hard to pick up. The dorsal (back) fin is contiguous with the caudal (tail) and anal fins. There are well-developed pectoral fins, but no pelvic (ventral) fins.

European Eel

Anguilla anguilla

Other names: Eel, Snig

Having bred at sea, the European Eel spends the rest of its life in flowing and standing fresh and brackish waters, although some remain at sea. It is a widespread, predatory species that feeds on a range of smaller fish and larger invertebrates. Individuals can remain cryptic, burying in soft sediment or inhabiting caves and dense stands of vegetation. Although they tend to hide away in deeper water and obstructions by day, European Eels become active at night, hunting at all depths. They have a dark body colour, from olive-green to black, but fading to paler on the belly. The European Eel population has declined rapidly over the last few years and, although still widespread, is now considered to be at high risk of extinction.

Critically Endangered	
Native	
UK BAP Priority Species	
Widespread but in decline	
Riverine, Still Water, Estuarine	
Max. length:	91 cm (36 inches)
Max. weight:	5·4 kg (12 lb)

Eels are not easily confused with other species, except perhaps the lampreys (*pages 119–122*), but are readily distinguished by the presence of jaws, paired pectoral fins and a single pair of gills.

Identification: The characteristic snake-like body of the European Eel appears scaleless, but is in fact covered in minute scales that are coated in thick slime. This makes the fish feel smooth to the touch. The dorsal (back) fin is contiguous with the caudal (tail) and anal fin. There are well-developed pectoral fins, but no pelvic (ventral) fins. The mouth is large and lacks barbels. European Eels are not known to hybridize with any other species.

Ecology: The European Eel has a remarkable life-cycle. Hatched from eggs assumed to be laid in the Sargasso Sea, a region in the middle of the North Atlantic Ocean bounded by ocean currents, the minute flattened larvae known as leptocephali drift on the Gulf Stream for two years before arriving on the European shoreline, where they metamorphose into small, transparent 'glass eels'. Some juveniles remain in estuaries and coastal waters whilst others ascend rivers and make their way, over land, to ponds, lakes, canals, and to other rivers and streams. Here they become darker and can live for up to twenty years or more. Late in the year, generally close to a full moon, maturing eels turn more silvery and run down rivers. They are capable of moving over land on moist nights to escape from enclosed waters. Now known as 'silver eels', they take to sea and migrate. It is assumed that they return to the Sargasso Sea to spawn, but tracking experiments have found that silver eels migrate southwards as far as the Azores, beyond which no further data from tags were recovered.

Conservation: European Eels can withstand moderate pollution but thrive best in good quality water. They particularly benefit from a diversity of habitats, which provides them not only with a variety of food items, but deep water refuges and other places in which to hide.

In the first decade of the 21st century, European Eel numbers have crashed by around 90%. The reasons for this are not fully understood but the species is clearly vulnerable to different threats during the many stages in its complex life-cycle, which is also incompletely understood. European Eels have further conservation importance as they are the preferred food for other species of concern, such as otter and bittern.

Lamprey family
Petromyzontidae

**3 British species
(all native; 2 of which have
a marine life-phase)**

The family Petromyzontidae comprises some 41 species of parasitic or non-parasitic, eel-like fishes across the world's temperate zones. Technically, the lampreys are not fish at all, since they lack jaws and possess only a cartilaginous skeleton. They also lack scales and paired fins.

The larval form of all lamprey species is slender and worm-like in appearance, and is known as an ammocoete. Ammocoetes are characterized by a line of circular gill openings behind the eye. They inhabit the edges of streams and the smaller headwaters of rivers where they remain buried and inconspicuous, filter-feeding or grazing on detritus.

Prior to spawning, ammocoete larvae metamorphose into adults. Immediately after metamorphosis, adult lampreys are usually shorter than their larvae, developing an eel-shaped body and two contiguous dorsal fins. Across the world, there are numerous examples of paired 'satellite' species of lamprey, including two of the three British species: the Brook Lamprey and the River Lamprey. The River Lamprey grows on and lives out its adult life at sea before returning to rivers to spawn, whereas the Brook Lamprey does not migrate but instead spawns shortly after metamorphosis. Some authorities believe that these paired 'satellite' species may not be true species at all, merely variants of single species exhibiting different life histories. There currently is no strong consensus on this matter and while research continues to unravel this mystery, the Brook Lamprey and the River Lamprey are considered as separate species.

The adult form of most lamprey species is parasitic, the fish attaching themselves to the sides of other fishes and feeding on their flesh, which they rasp off with circular rows of teeth in the mouth disk, and on their body fluids.

All species of lamprey, both marine and freshwater, breed in fresh waters. Parent fish run up rivers, building a nest in gravel or sand and then dying after spawning. All lampreys require clean, flowing water, but also marginal shallows containing organically enriched mud in which ammocoetes burrow and from which they can filter-feed. Pollution, excessive river management including dredging, impoundments and loss of habitat diversity all pose significant threats to lamprey species, with obstructions of many types posing a particular problem during migration.

Brook Lamprey   *Lampetra planeri*

Other names: Planer's Lamprey, European Brook Lamprey, 'Nine Eyes', Pride, Sandpride, Brookie

Brook Lampreys are small, elongated fishes that spend most of their lives as ammocoete larvae (see *page 121*). Prior to spawning, the ammocoetes metamorphose into adults, which then live only short lives before spawning and dying.

Identification: Brook Lamprey ammocoetes are rarely more than 15 cm (6") in length, and are toothless and blind. The two dorsal fins are joined into a contiguous fin along the back, merging into the tail fin with only a conspicuous dip. The fins for the most part lack pigment.

Least Concern	
Bern Convention (App. III)	
Habitats Directive (Ann. II)	
Native	
Localized	
Riverine	
Max. length:	20 cm (8 inches)
Max. weight:	57 g (2 oz)

Adult Brook Lampreys are eel-shaped with a grey or brownish, often slightly metallic body colour that grades to white or yellowish on the belly. They have a pair of functional eyes and a small sucking disc, though the teeth are blunt and weak as adult fish do not feed. Brook Lampreys also have seven small, round gill openings on either side of the head, which were once thought to be additional eyes (hence the regional alternative name).

Ecology: Brook Lampreys spend their entire lives in flowing fresh water. They are non-parasitic and non-migratory, spending five years as filter-feeding ammocoete larva before metamorphosing in the autumn through to early spring into the adult form, at which point the larvae have reached a length of 12–18 cm (5–7"). The adult does not feed. Consequently, the gut atrophies (wastes away) and, after spawning on sand or fine gravel

> The Brook Lamprey is the most common of three British lamprey species. Unlike the other two species, 'brookies' are non-migratory, spending their whole lives in streams. The other species are larger, River Lamprey reaching 30–40 cm (12–16") and Sea Lamprey (*page 122*) 50–120 cm (20–47"). Brook and River Lamprey ammocoetes are indistinguishable and both lack the extensive pigment of Sea Lamprey ammocoetes.

during springtime of the year in which it matures, the adult Brook Lamprey dies.

Conservation: The conservation threats faced by Brook Lampreys are as described for all lamprey species, including pollution, excessive river management, impoundments and loss of habitat diversity.

River Lamprey   *Lampetra fluviatalis*

Other names: Lampern, Juneba, Stone Grig, Lamper Eel

River Lampreys are elongated, eel-like fishes. The early part of the life cycle is spent as a filter-feeding ammocoete larva in river silts before metamorphosing into the parasitic adult form. Adult River Lampreys inhabit the estuaries of large rivers, attaching themselves with their rasping mouthparts to the flanks of other fishes (particularly herrings, flounders and sprats) and feeding on their body fluids and tissues. River Lampreys return to rivers to breed.

Identification: The shape and characteristics of River Lampreys are typical of all parasitic lampreys, lacking lower jaws, bones, scales and paired fins. River Lamprey ammocoetes are rarely longer than 15 cm (6"). They are also toothless, blind and largely lack pigment, and are otherwise physically indistinguishable from those of the Brook Lamprey.

Adults River Lampreys possess a pair of functional eyes, behind which are seven small round gill openings on either side of the head. Their body colour is generally a drab slate-grey on the back, though sometimes brownish, grading to white or yellowish on the belly.

Least Concern	
Bern Convention (App. III)	
Habitats Directive (Ann. II & V)	
Native	
UK BAP Priority Species	
Localized	
Riverine, Estuarine	
Max. length:	50 cm (20 inches)
Max. weight:	150 g (11 oz)

> It is possible to confuse the River Lamprey with other lamprey species, Brook Lamprey (*page 119*) and Sea Lamprey (*page 122*) in both the larval and adult life-stages. Sea Lamprey ammocoetes have extensive pigment unlike the larvae of either of the other species. As adults, River Lampreys are intermediate in size between the Brook Lamprey, which is much smaller at only 12–20 cm (5–8"), and the Sea Lamprey, which is substantially larger at 50–120 cm (20–48").

Ecology: The ammocoete larvae of the River Lamprey live for around three to five years in the margins of flowing fresh water, thereafter metamorphosing and descending rivers to take to sea for their adult parasitic phase.

ABOVE: *The Brook Lamprey does not feed during the brief adult phase of its life-cycle.*
INSET: *The weak sucking disc mouthparts of a Brook Lamprey.*

Head of an adult River Lamprey (top), ammocoete larvae (centre) and adult Brook Lamprey (bottom)

Adults return to fresh waters after one or two years, running rivers in October to December and ceasing to feed. Spawning occurs between March and May, adults working in groups to move stones to create spawning depressions. The sticky eggs adhere to the substrate. There is no parental care, River Lampreys dying shortly after spawning.

Conservation: The conservation threats faced by River Lampreys are as described for all lamprey species, including pollution, excessive river management, impoundments and loss of habitat diversity.

Sea Lamprey   *Petromyzon marinus*

Other names: Marine Lamprey, Lamprey Eel

The Sea Lamprey is the largest British lamprey. It occurs widely in the north-east Atlantic from Norway to northern Africa, the western Atlantic from Labrador to the Gulf of Mexico, and as landlocked populations in North America's Great Lakes. It is elongated and eel-like, rounded in cross-section but more laterally compressed towards the tail. Adults inhabit coastal and marine waters, feeding parasitically on the flanks of various fish species with their rasping mouthparts, and returning to rivers to breed.

Least Concern	
Bern Convention (App. III)	
Habitats Directive (Ann. II)	
Native	
UK BAP Priority Species	
Localized	
Riverine, Estuarine	
Max. length:	120 cm (47 inches)
Max. weight:	2·5 kg (5 lb 8 oz)

The Sea Lamprey is considerably larger than the River Lamprey (*page 120*) at 30–40 cm (12–16") and the Brook Lamprey (*page 119*) at 12–20 cm (5–8").

Identification: The ammocoete larvae of Sea Lamprey rarely exceed 15 cm (6"), and are toothless and blind. However, unlike those of the River Lamprey (*page 120*) and Brook Lamprey (*page 119*), Sea Lamprey ammocoetes have characteristic extensive black pigmentation almost to the lower surface of the top lip, into the caudal fin (tail) and in bands on the flanks extending to, or almost to, the ventral surface. Like all parasitic lampreys, adult Sea Lampreys lack lower jaws, bones, scales or paired fins, but have rasping, sucking mouthparts armed with horny teeth. They also possess a relatively large pair of eyes, behind which are seven small, round gill openings on either side of the head. Adult body colour varies from mottled greys and browns grading to lighter tones beneath.

Ecology: Sea Lamprey ammocoetes spend around five years burrowing in soft, organically-enriched silt in the margins or deeper water of rivers, filter-feeding and also grazing on algae, small invertebrates and organic matter adjacent to their burrows. After metamorphosis, Sea Lampreys take to sea to live as parasitic adults. They return to rivers between May and June to spawn after one or two years at sea, at which time they cease to feed. Males arrive on the spawning gravels before the females, moving stones to build redds into which females lay hundreds of thousands of sticky eggs, after which the adults die.

Conservation: Although generally considered a pest in North America due to the damage they inflict on fish species valued for sport or food, Sea Lampreys are increasingly scarce in the British Isles where they face the range of conservation threats described for all lamprey species, including pollution, excessive river management, impoundments and loss of habitat diversity.

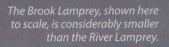

The Brook Lamprey, shown here to scale, is considerably smaller than the River Lamprey.

ABOVE: *The River Lamprey has a parasitic adult life phase, occupying estuaries before returning to rivers to spawn and die.* BELOW: *The Sea Lamprey is the largest of the British lamprey species, growing up to 120 cm (47 inches) in length.*

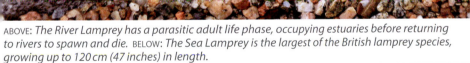

123

Whilst not true freshwater fishes, a number of marine fishes enter estuaries and move further up rivers into fresh waters, particularly during the summer months. These 'marine visitor' species are considered briefly in this section, including three species of mullet, the European Seabass, the Flounder, the Smelt and the Sand-smelt. All are common and widespread and, with one exception, are categorized by IUCN as Least Concern. The exception is the Sand-smelt, which is Not Evaluated.

Silversides family
Atherinidae

1 British species (native; estuarine)

The family Atherinidae comprises 165 species found in fresh, brackish and marine waters in both tropical and temperate waters.

Sand-smelt

Atherina presbyter

The Sand-smelt, also known as the Little Sand Smelt, is a shoaling species of inshore and coastal marine waters. It also favours estuaries and can penetrate the lower reaches of rivers.

| Max. length: | 20 cm (8 inches) |
| Max. weight: | 100 g (5 oz) |

Sand-smelt have an intense silvery line, often outlined in black, from head to tail along a silvery, elongated and laterally compressed body that is covered in relatively large scales. They lack a true lateral line but there are 52–57 scales in longitudinal series. These fishes have a large pair of pectoral fins and two widely separated dorsal fins, the first with 7–9 flexible spines and the second with soft rays. The eyes are large, the eye diameter being equal to the length of the snout, and the mouth is upturned.

These fishes are gregarious, favouring low-salinity water and feeding primarily on zooplankton, particularly small crustaceans and fish larvae. Isolated freshwater populations are known in several Italian and Spanish lakes and in some lower river reaches around the Mediterranean, but not in Britain and Ireland. Sand-smelt reproduce in spring and summer, favouring intertidal pools and coastal lagoons, and can live for up to 4 years.

Smelt family
Osmeridae

1 British species (native; estuarine)

The family Osmeridae comprises 13 species of freshwater, brackish and marine fishes, with maxillary and premaxillary teeth and an adipose fin between the dorsal fin and the tail. They are found across the Northern Hemisphere in both the Atlantic and Pacific Oceans.

Smelt

Osmerus eperianus

Max. length:	30 cm (12 inches)
Max. weight:	230 g (8 oz)

The Smelt, also known as the Sparling, is the only member of its family to be recorded in British waters. It is rarely found far from the coast, and has a relatively restricted distribution in or close to estuaries. In larger estuaries, the Smelt is often resident and it sometimes enters the lower reaches of rivers.

Smelt have a single dorsal fin that lacks spines but is supported by 9–12 soft rays. The head and snout are pointed, the lower jaw reaching to the hind margin of the eye and also projecting a little beyond the tip of the upper jaw. Smelt possess both premaxillary and maxillary teeth. The teeth in the lower jaw are larger than those of the upper, and there are strong teeth on the tongue. There is also an incomplete lateral line, and a pronounced silvery stripe runs along the bright flanks. The heads of male Smelt may grow numerous small tubercles as they enter more dilute brackish waters to spawn. Another characteristic feature of Smelt is that living and freshly caught fish smell of cucumber.

The Smelt is listed as a species of fresh waters in The Reverend W. Houghton's 1879 book *British Fresh-Water Fishes*, and some freshwater Smelt populations do occur elsewhere in Europe. However, although British Smelt occasionally spawn in lower rivers between February and April, the adult fish then return to sea and the young fish move down into estuaries after hatching, where they remain throughout the summer. Smelt are carnivorous, preying on small fish and larger invertebrates, and are known to live for up to ten years.

Righteye flounder family
Pleuronectidae

1 British species (native; estuarine)

The family Pleuronectidae comprises 93 species of predominantly marine flatfish spread across the Arctic, Atlantic, Indian and Pacific Oceans.

Flounder

Platichthys flesus

The Flounder is a common species around Britain's shores and is the only species of British flatfish that enters fresh waters.

Max. length:	30 cm (12 inches)
Max. weight:	2·6 kg (5 lb 12 oz)

Both eyes are normally on the right side of the body, and the fins lack spines, including the dorsal fin that extends onto the head. The pigmented upperside of the body is capable of remarkable colour changes to match the muddy and sandy bottom sediments of a river or the sea bed. The lateral line is straight, but slightly rounded over the pectoral fins.

Flounders spawn in deep offshore waters during the spring, but throughout the summer months routinely move in to regions of estuaries with fresh water outflows and may penetrate upstream into fully fresh water. Flounders can live in fresh water for some time and regularly occur in the lower reaches of rivers. Typically, they enter the intertidal zone with the incoming tide, and then move with the rising water up into estuaries to feed on benthic invertebrates and small fishes.

Temperate bass family
Moronidae

1 British species
(native; mainly marine but may penetrate
up rivers, especially in summer)

The family Moronidae comprises six species of bass found in coastal areas from Atlantic and Gulf of Mexico drainages of North America to those of Europe and northern Africa. Only one species occurs commonly in waters around the British Isles.

European Seabass

Dicentrarchus labrax

The European Seabass is the only member of its family regularly found in the British Isles, where it is usually simply referred to as the 'Bass', or sometimes as the 'Sea Dace', perhaps

| Max. length: | 60 cm (24 inches) |
| Max. weight: | 8·6 kg (19 lb) |

due to its swift and lithe swimming and silvery appearance. It has a graceful, elongated body that is silvery-grey to bluish on the back, silver on the sides, and white on the belly, sometimes tinged with yellow. The lateral line is complete, with between 62 and 74 (usually 70) small scales, but it does not extend onto the caudal (tail) fin. The jaws lack teeth, but a band of small vomerine teeth is present on the front part of the roof of the mouth, serving to hold prey – mainly fish but also larger invertebrates – once captured. This fish has two dorsal fins: the first comprises 8–10 spines and the second has a single spine behind which are 10–13 soft rays. There are also two spines on the rear of the gill cover (or operculum).

Bass are notably migratory in behaviour, moving northwards and inshore with warming weather in spring and retreating southwards again in the winter. They are also prone to migrating into brackish and sometimes into fresh water during summer excursions.

Mullet family
Mugilidae

3 British species
**(native; mainly marine but penetrate
up rivers, particularly in summer)**

The mullets comprise 72 species of predominantly marine and estuarine fishes. They possess two dorsal fins: one that is short and supported by four stout spines; and the other that is soft and well separated. The pectoral fins are situated high on the flanks. Even when present, the lateral line is barely visible. The mouth usually lacks teeth, although small teeth may sometimes be present. These schooling fishes have extremely long intestines to aid digestion of their diet of fine algae including diatoms and detritus from bottom sediments, which they graze with their rubbery lips. Three species are found in British estuaries in the summer, some penetrating further up river systems. All three breed at sea during the late summer or winter, laying pelagic and non-adhesive eggs, the juveniles drifting inshore and often inhabiting estuaries. The mullets are largely inshore species in the summer months.

Golden Grey Mullet   *Liza aurata*

This widespread species is found in the eastern Atlantic from Scotland to Cape Verde. The pectoral fins are long, reaching well past the rear of the eye orbit and generally half way

Max. length:	50 cm (20 inches)
Max. weight:	1·4 kg (3 lb)

across the eye when folded forward, and there is no black spot at the base of the pectoral fin. A golden spot is present on the gill cover, giving the species its common name. The mouth is small, and the upper lip is thin (always less than half the eye diameter) and lacks papillae. It feeds on small benthic organisms, detritus and occasionally on insects and plankton, and breeds at sea from July to November.

Thin-lipped Grey Mullet   *Liza ramada*

Similar to the Thick-lipped Grey Mullet, with a large head that is flattened above the eyes. The mouth is small and the upper lip is thin (always less than half the eye diameter),

Max. length:	60 cm (24 inches)
Max. weight:	3·2 kg (7 lb)

lacking papillae. The snout is short and blunt, and the scales are large. The pectoral fins are short, barely reaching the rear of the eye orbit when folded forward. The dorsal sides and flanks are grey in colour, fading to pale or white on the ventral side. This mullet can tolerate mildly polluted water. Spawning takes place at sea near the coast during gatherings between September and February.

Thick-lipped Grey Mullet   *Chelon labrosus*

Enters brackish lagoons and fresh waters during the summer when it migrates northwards as waters warm. The upper lip is thick, its greatest depth equal to at least half

Max. length:	75 cm (30 inches)
Max. weight:	6·4 kg (14 lb)

the eye diameter, and several rows of small, dark papillae are present on its lower border. Feeding mainly on benthic diatoms, epiphytic algae, small invertebrates and detritus, it grows only slowly, and can live for up to 30 years. This species breeds at sea during the late summer into winter, from late July to November.

▲ *Golden Grey Mullet*

Thin-lipped Grey Mullet ▲   ▼ *Thick-lipped Grey Mullet*

Fishy fantasies

This section covers freshwater fish species that are not now considered to be 'real' species.

In the species account for Brown Trout (see *page 84*), reference was made to the fact that this variable species was formerly thought to have been many different species, including the sea-going Sea Trout and the Ferox – the deep-water piscivore with fearsome jaws. However, in the Reverend W. Houghton's classic 1879 book *British Fresh-Water Fishes*, the fish we know today as the Brown Trout *Salmo trutta* was listed as follows, differentiated by variations in colour and morphology:

Salmon Trout *Salmo truta*
Sewen *Salmo cambricus*
Bull Trout *Salmo eriox*
Galway Sea Trout *Salmo gallivensis*
Short-headed Salmon *Salmo brachypoma*
Silvery Salmon *Salmo argenteus*

Common Trout *Salmo fario*
Black-finned Trout *Salmo nigripinnis*
Loch Stennis Trout *Salmo orcadensis*
Lochleven Trout *Salmo levenensis*
Gillaroo Trout *Salmo stomachius*
Great Lake Trout *Salmo ferox*

We have also 'lost' other apparent freshwater fish species that were, as we now perceive them, misclassified. Species considered in this brief overview include the Graining, the Azurine and the Dobule, all three of which were considered to be cyprinids (members of the carp and minnow family Cyprinidae). The illustrations of these fishes reproduced here were painted by A.F. Lydon and are taken from Houghton's book.

Graining

The Graining was classified as *Leuciscus lancastriensis* in William Yarrell's 1836 text *The History of British Fishes*, based on a single specimen that he had examined from a small tributary of the Mersey near Formby. This is hardly sound, replicable science, at least by modern standards. A description of the Graining taken from the 1843 book *The diary of A. J. Lane: With a Description of those Fishes to be Found in British Fresh Waters* notes that:

> "*In form somewhat like a Dace, but much rounder in the belly, tail deeply forked, top of the head and back a sort of drab coming down the sides and terminating rather suddenly; beneath this and the belly much lighter, eyes whitish, cheeks white, or yellowish, scales much smaller than in the Dace.*
> "*This fish is believed to be confined to the waters of Lancashire. They are said to rise very freely to flys and also take baits as for Roach.*"

The Graining not only looked like a brownish-tinged Dace, but in fact was exactly that.

The species vanished from scientific and popular discussion shortly after publication of Houghton's book. British ichthyologist C. Tate Regan finally and definitively dismissed the separate identity of the Graining in his 1911 work *The Freshwater Fishes of the British Isles*.

Graining are described in a number of early works on freshwater fishes, but are in fact merely misclassified dace. (Original painting by A. F. Lydon, published in the Reverend W. Houghton's 1879 book British Fresh-Water Fishes.*)*

Azurine are another fictitious 'species', perhaps reflecting the keenness of early naturalists to discover new species. (Original painting by A. F. Lydon, published in the Reverend W. Houghton's 1879 book British Fresh-Water Fishes.)

Azurine

Another product of the imagination of those with fishy interests prior to and during Houghton's day, also lovingly recorded and illustrated in *British Fresh-Water Fishes,* was the Azurine. The Azurine (*Leuciscus caeruleus* Yarrell 1837 and formerly known as *Cyprinus caeruleus* Yarrell, 1833) was also known as the Blue Roach or Lemon-finned Rudd. It was reputedly found in very limited localities within the town of Knowsley, Lancashire. A description of the Azurine from the 1843 book *The Diary of A. J. Lane: With a Description of those Fishes to be found in British Fresh Waters,* records that the Azurine is:

> "In shape like a Roach but rather longer, tail long and forked; head, back and sides slate color passing into silvery white."
> "Never exceed one lb in weight; is hardy and tenacious of life."

In *British Fresh-Water Fishes* (1879), the Reverend W. Houghton notes, after having examined many preserved specimens of this fish, that:

> "The Rudd, like fish generally, is subject to variety, and it would appear that the Azurine, or Blue Roach, first described by Yarrell under the name of Leuciscus caeruleus (Linn. Soc. Trans, vol. xvii. p. i. p. 8.), is merely a variety of the Rudd."

The Azurine was identified by William Yarrell from an anomalous fish with a bluish sheen, apparently misidentified as a discrete species. Other fish scientists also agreed that this fish was a variety of the Rudd, and specimens were, perhaps unsurprisingly, no longer subsequently found in the Knowsley area. The Azurine is now considered to be simply a synonym for the Rudd *Scardinius erythrophthalmus.*

The Dobule

The Dobule, or Dobule Roach, was another fish classified by the zoologist William Yarrell (1784–1856), once again in a hardly scientific manner from a single specimen. The fact that the identification was from one specimen only, taken from the brackish waters of the Thames estuary, should really have encouraged Yarrell to be a little more tentative in declaring it a new British freshwater fish species. In his consideration of this fish in *British Fresh-Water Fishes,* one rather gets the feeling that the Reverend W. Houghton had his doubts about this fish too, as he writes:

> "The Dobule Roach, a single specimen of which Yarrell took with the mouth of a White-bait net in the Thames below Woolwich, and which is regarded by Günther as a small Dace, is thus in its principal characteristics described by Yarrell…"

The 'species' was once thought to exist elsewhere across Europe. Initially, enjoying the scientific name *Cyprinus dobula* Linnaeus 1758, the fish was later reclassified as *Leuciscus dobula* (Linnaeus, 1758) reflecting its dace-like affinities. The next move was to realise that the dace-like Dobule was, in reality, a Dace.

Conservation and legislation

Many of the freshwater fishes of Britain and Ireland are the subject of nature conservation concern. For some, such as Arctic Charr and Atlantic Salmon, declining populations demand management action. Other non-native species, such as Topmouth Gudgeon and Black Bullhead, pose a threat to native species and ecosystems, and therefore their reintroduction to the fresh waters of the British Isles or their further spread needs to be strictly controlled. This is essential as, in addition to their roles in cycling food, energy and parasites, freshwater fishes are an important part of freshwater ecosystems at all levels in the food chain. Their conservation, or in the case of problematic species, appropriate management, is vital for the future of healthy and sustainable managed watercourses and other wetland habitats.

Fishes of direct conservation importance

The IUCN Red List

The International Union for Conservation of Nature (IUCN) Red List of Threatened Species, also known as The IUCN Red List or Red Data List, is a comprehensive and regularly updated inventory of the global conservation status of species of plants and animals. Both global and regional lists are maintained, classifying species according to extinction risk based on established criteria. These criteria include the rate of decline, population size, area of geographic distribution, and degree of population and distribution fragmentation.

The purpose of the Red List is to communicate conservation issues to the public and policy-makers. Species are categorized as either Extinct (EX); Extinct in the Wild (EW); Critically Endangered (CR); Endangered (EN); Vulnerable (VU); Near Threatened (NT); Least Concern (LC); Data Deficient (DD); or Not Evaluated (NE).

The term 'threatened' is a grouping of the Critically Endangered, Endangered and Vulnerable categories.

Many British freshwater fish species are classified as Least Concern, though the wild form of the Common Carp is classified as Vulnerable. Two species, the European Eel and the Common Sturgeon, are now listed as Critically Endangered. The coregonids (whitefish) are particularly threatened globally, with Houting listed as Extinct. Although treated as local populations of the European Whitefish *Corgonus lavaretus* in this guide, the Red

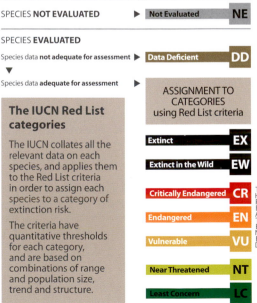

The IUCN species category assignment process

SPECIES **NOT EVALUATED** ▶ Not Evaluated **NE**

SPECIES **EVALUATED**

Species data **not adequate for assessment** ▶ Data Deficient **DD**

▼

Species data **adequate for assessment** ▶ ASSIGNMENT TO CATEGORIES using Red List criteria

The IUCN Red List categories

The IUCN collates all the relevant data on each species, and applies them to the Red List criteria in order to assign each species to a category of extinction risk.

The criteria have quantitative thresholds for each category, and are based on combinations of range and population size, trend and structure.

Extinct **EX**

Extinct in the Wild **EW**

Critically Endangered **CR**

Endangered **EN**

Vulnerable **VU**

Near Threatened **NT**

Least Concern **LC**

THREATENED

List recognizes as separate the Gwyniad (Critically Endangered) and the Powan (Vulnerable). Despite its scarcity in the British Isles, the Vendace is evaluated as Least Concern across its natural range.

Some species are Not Evaluated due to a lack of scientific information. These include the native Sand-smelt, but also a number of species introduced to British fresh waters (Rainbow Trout, Goldfish, Grass Carp, Topmouth Gudgeon, Pumpkinseed Sunfish and Black Bullhead).

The Bern Convention

The Bern Convention on the Conservation of European Wildlife and Natural Habitats 1979, which is generally referred to as simply the Bern Convention (or Berne Convention), came into force in 1982.

Its aims are to: conserve wild flora and fauna and their natural habitats; promote co-operation between states; monitor and control endangered and vulnerable species; and help with the provision of assistance concerning legal and scientific issues. The Bern Convention led to the creation in 1998 of the Emerald Network of Areas of Special Conservation Interest (ASCIs) throughout the territory of the parties to the Convention, which operates alongside the EU Natura 2000 programme. It also provides for the monitoring and control of endangered species, and the provision of assistance concerning legal and scientific issues. Four appendices, each regularly updated by Expert Groups, set out particular species for protection.

Appendix I addresses strictly protected flora species, and therefore does not directly concern fish.

Appendix II lists strictly protected fauna species. Of the British freshwater fish species, only the Common Sturgeon is listed.

Appendix III is concerned with species that are regulated but the exploitation of which is controlled in accordance with the Directive. These species include:
　River Lamprey
　Brook Lamprey
　Sea Lamprey
　Allis Shad
　Twaite Shad
　Grayling
　Atlantic Salmon
　Spined Loach
　Sunbleak / Belica (a troublesome introduced species in the UK)
　Wels Catfish (a species introduced to British waters)
　Bitterling (a species introduced to British waters)

Appendix IV lists the following prohibited means and methods of killing, capture and other forms of exploitation:
　Explosives
　Firearms
　Poisons
　Anaesthetics
　Electricity with alternating current
　Artificial light sources

The European Union Habitats Directive

The European Union (EU) Habitats Directive (Council Directive 92/43/EEC on the Conservation of Natural Habitats and of Wild Fauna and Flora) was adopted in 1992 as one of the cornerstones, together with the EU Birds Directive, of Europe's nature conservation policy. The Habitats Directive, including subsequent amendments, comprises two pillars: the Natura 2000 network of protected sites, and a strict system of species protection. One thousand animal and plant species and over 200 'habitat types' of European importance are covered by the Habitats Directive. The Habitats Directive is also the means by which the EU meets its obligations under the Bern Convention. The Directive thereby promotes the maintenance of biodiversity by requiring

Member States to take measures to maintain or restore natural habitats and wild species listed in the Annexes to the Directive at a favourable conservation status through robust protection measures that also take account of economic, social and cultural requirements, as well as regional and local characteristics. These Annexes are:

Annex I: Natural habitat types of community interest whose conservation requires the designation of Special Areas of Conservation (SAC). This comprises a list of habitat types, some of which are relevant to various British freshwater fish species.

Annex II: Animal and plant species of community interest whose conservation requires the designation of Special Areas of Conservation (SAC). These include (with some regional exclusions):
River Lamprey
Brook Lamprey
Sea Lamprey
Common Sturgeon
Allis Shad
Twaite Shad
Atlantic Salmon
Bitterling *(an introduced species in the UK)*
Spined Loach
Bullhead

Annex III: Criteria for selecting sites eligible for identification as sites of community importance and designation as Special Areas of Conservation (SAC). This includes site selection based on, amongst other criteria, the needs of species listed in Annex II.

Annex IV: Animal and plant species of community interest in need of strict protection. This includes the following British fishes (with regional exemptions for some species):
Common Sturgeon
Houting (the IUCN has classified this species as Extinct)

Annex V: Animal and plant species of community interest whose taking in the wild and exploitation may be subject to management measures. This Annex includes:
River Lamprey
Allis Shad
Twaite shad
Grayling
All species of *Coregonus* except Houting, thus including:
Vendace
European Whitefish (including Gwyniad, Powan, Pollan and Schelly)
Atlantic Salmon
Barbel

Annex VI: Prohibited methods and means of capture and killing and modes of transport:
Poison
Explosives

In the United Kingdom the Directive has been transposed into law by The Conservation (Natural Habitats, &c.) Regulations 1994, and The Conservation of Habitats and Species Regulations 2010 consolidating various amendments. In Scotland, the Habitats Directive is transposed through a combination of the Habitats Regulations 2010 (in relation to reserved matters) and the UK's 1994 Regulations. The Conservation (Natural Habitats, &c) Regulations (Northern Ireland) 1995 (as amended) transpose the Habitats Directive in relation to Northern Ireland. The Offshore Marine Conservation (Natural Habitats etc.) Regulations 2007 (as amended) address EU Habitats Directive requirements for UK offshore waters (from 12 nautical miles from the coast out to 200 nautical miles or to the limit of the UK Continental Shelf Designated Area).

The Wildlife and Countryside Act 1981

The Wildlife and Countryside Act 1981 (as subsequently amended) is the means by which the UK implemented the EU Birds Directive (Directive 2009/147/EC on the Conservation of Wild Birds) but also consolidates various other forms of protection of wildlife. The Act gives protection to native species (especially those under threat), controls the release of non-native species, enhances the protection of Sites of Special Scientific Interest (SSSIs) and builds upon the rights of way rules in the National Parks and Access to the Countryside Act 1949. It comprises 4 parts and is supported by 17 schedules, the relevant ones being:

Schedule 5: Animals which are protected (in England and Wales)
  Allis Shad
  Twaite Shad
  Common Sturgeon
  Vendace
  European Whitefish

Schedule 9: Animals and plants to which section 14 applies. (Section 14 relates to the "Introduction of new species etc.".)
  Bitterling
  Pumpkinseed Sunfish
  Wels Catfish
  Zander

Schedule 10: Amendment of the Endangered Species (Import and Export) Act 1976. This affects a number of fish and other species prohibited from import into the UK.

The UK Biodiversity Action Plan

The UK Biodiversity Action Plan (UK BAP), published in 1994, is the UK Government's response to the Convention on Biological Diversity (CBD) to which the UK became a signatory at the 1992 Rio de Janeiro 'Earth Summit'. The CBD called for the development and enforcement of national strategies and associated action plans to identify, conserve and protect existing biological diversity, and to enhance it wherever possible.

Fishes listed under the UK BAP include:
  Common Sturgeon *(not in Wales)*
  Allis Shad
  Twaite Shad
  European Eel
  Spined Loach *(not in Scotland, Wales or Northern Ireland)*
  Vendace *(not in Wales or Northern Ireland)*
  European Whitefish (including Powan, Pollan, Gwyniad and Schelly)
  River Lamprey
  Burbot *(though noted as extinct in England, Wales Scotland and Northern Ireland)*
  Smelt (Sparling)
  Sea Lamprey
  Atlantic Salmon
  Brown Trout
  Arctic Charr *(not in Northern Ireland)*

Fishes of value to other species of conservation concern

As fishes serve many important roles in food chains at all trophic levels, they play an important part in the functioning and resilience of aquatic and associated ecosystems. Some are also an important food source for species of conservation concern. A good example is the Rudd, which favours standing and slow-moving waters, some of which also comprise the reedbed fringe habitat favoured by the Great Bittern, one of Britain's rarest birds that is included in the UK BAP. The European Eel, a fish species now listed as Critically Endangered on The IUCN Red List, is also a favoured food for BAP species including the European Otter and birds covered by the EU Birds Directive and the UK's Wildlife and Countryside Act 1981, including Great Cormorant and Grey Heron.

Problematic invasive freshwater fish species

Many fishes introduced beyond their natural range can be problematic, disrupting ecosystems and the beneficial services they provide to people. The Common Carp is a particular offender, having been introduced beyond its native range (the drainage basins of the Black, Caspian and Aral Seas) into all parts of the world except the Arctic and Antarctic, and frequently profoundly changing the nature of aquatic ecosystems. The Common Carp continues frequently to alter substantially the balance and properties of British waters when introduced, though many now regard the species as naturalized since it was introduced into the UK from the 15th century. The same disruptive potential is seen when native species, such as the Barbel, are transferred from rivers in which they are naturally present (eastern drainage basins entering the North Sea from the Thames northwards to the many rivers converging on the Humber estuary) into rivers in which the species has not co-evolved.

However, it is to more recent alien introductions that most attention has been paid. Fortunately, the control of potentially alien invasive fish species is considered with rather more foresight than it is for plants, for which controls are generally only put in place when adverse effects have become apparent and may already be irreversible.

Threats from foreign freshwater fish species to the balance and integrity of our freshwater ecosystems are assessed on the basis of their potential to escape and form self-perpetuating populations in British waters. The Import of Live Fish (England and Wales) Act 1980, or ILFA for short, is the primary legislation. In 1998, the Prohibition of Keeping or Release of Live Fish (Specified Species) Order was also introduced in an effort to reduce the number of fish species illegally introduced into fresh waters in England and Wales, adding further species to the list of those initially scheduled under ILFA. These legal instruments list a number of temperate freshwater fishes believed to pose a threat to the environment owing to their potential for forming self-sustaining populations and so perturbing the balance of native ecosystems. The legislation stipulates that suppliers need a licence to sell listed species, and fish-keepers also require a special licence to keep some of the scheduled fishes. The Prohibition of Keeping or Release (Specified Species) Scotland Order 2003 is largely similar to the Order for England and Wales.

Fishing closed seasons

Although the origins of angling (fishing with a hook) probably have their roots in the capture of fish for food, concerns for the wellbeing of fish stocks has characterized many recreational developments over recent centuries. The statutory closed season for coarse fish species was introduced in the UK by the Fresh Water Fisheries Act of 1878, recognizing that, despite its inherently harmless nature, increased fish mortality resulted from continuing to fish throughout the breeding season. Informed by the fact that British coarse fish breed principally between mid-March and mid-June, this Act set the established closed season for coarse angling between 15th March and 15th June to protect both fishes and the sport of angling.

This closed season remains in force today on the rivers of England and Wales, though has been relaxed on still waters (subject to the discretion of landowners and nature conservation agencies). No such closed season for coarse fishing exists in Scotland or Northern Ireland, where controls on angling are at the discretion of landowners.

Conservation of salmon and trout stocks also underlies angling closed seasons, though these are variable across the country reflecting local breeding patterns. For example, the salmon angling open season starts on 17th January and runs through to 2nd October on the River Itchen (Hampshire), which also has a Sea Trout angling season running from 1st March to 31st October. However, for the River Axe (Devon), the salmon season does not start until 15th May, running through to 31st October, with Sea Trout angling permitted from 15th April to 31st October.

In Scotland, the wild trout fishing season generally starts on 15th of March and continues to 30th September with some variations, though in Aberdeenshire and the Highlands the season generally starts on 1st April to give the trout a couple more weeks to return to good condition after the colder winter further north. On the Tay, Nith and Tweed river systems, the trout season extends to 6th October, and there are further local variations. The Scottish salmon angling season is more variable, commencing as early as 11th January (to 30th September) on the Carron, Cassley, Evlyx, Helmsdale, Shin and Oykel and as late as 15th June (to 15th October) on the Grimistra.

Similar locally adapted closed seasons are applied as conditions of licences for commercial netting and other forms of fishing.

Catch-and-release

Marking the transition of angling from a means of gathering food to a recreational activity informed by stock conservation concerns, catch-and-release fishing has become widespread. Coarse fisheries have been generally run on a catch-and-release basis for many years, at least since the Second World War, but this ethos has been slower to take root in game angling. However, concerns about stocks of salmon in particular, have given rise to a significant shift in opinion in attitudes and practice throughout the first decade of the current century. This is enforced regionally by byelaws.

For example, the Spring Byelaws, brought in by the Environment Agency in 1998, prohibit the killing of salmon before 16th June to protect early season stock. These early season fish are generally larger, multi-sea-winter fish that have stayed at sea for two or three years before returning to breed.

Surveys reveal that, despite widespread abhorrence of compulsory 'catch-and-release' byelaws at their inception, anglers' attitudes to conservation had changed so markedly by 2008 that there was a high degree of support to keep the initiative alive for a further ten years. Even those rivers with an arguable surplus of early running salmon, such as the Tyne, voted to keep to the byelaws, mainly due to concerns that the river would be inundated by anglers trying to catch a springer 'for the pot' should this river alone be granted dispensation.

Good fish care is of course essential but survival rates after capture by anglers is very high and ensures that released fish can continue to pass on their genes. The release of fish also contributes to sustainable angling tourism industries, which may be locally very significant.

Stocking

The stocking of fish in British waters has been an established practice over many centuries, with our fish fauna being perhaps the most disturbed of all taxonomic groups. This may have involved introductions of species initially for aquaculture and food purposes, which has seen the Common Carp introduced into British waters and indeed many waters across the world, often with severe environmental consequences. This practice continues today to serve a lucrative angling industry. Other species have been moved for similar purposes beyond their native ranges, including, for example, Barbel and Grayling that are now found in many British rivers despite being naturally distributed towards the south and east of England.

Stocking of fish can have worrying conservation implications. For example, introduced species can become established and compete with locally adapted species (as is the case with Barbel). They can also modify the ecosystem through their feeding habits (frequently observed world-wide with Common Carp introductions) or prevent the breeding of native species (a major concern with introduced Topmouth Gudgeon and Sunbleak). Introduced fish can also carry novel diseases (a major concern in transfers of farmed salmon) or unwanted 'passengers', such as other invasive fish species or problem plants (such as New Zealand Pigmyweed *Crassula helmsii*) or animals (including the Signal Crayfish *Pacifastacus leniusculus*).

However, stocking of trout, significantly often including the non-native Rainbow Trout, can be a positive conservation measure when angling pressure would otherwise deplete natural stocks. Stocking is of course no panacea, potentially giving rise to many of the introduction-related problems discussed above but also risking the dilution of localized genetic strains of trout and salmon. It is for this reason that policy changes are encouraging a progressive transition either to stocking with native provenance trout, or else with increasing proportions of sterile (generally triploid) Brown or Rainbow Trout to avoid genetic impacts upon native stocks.

Some stock transfer operations directly support conservation goals. For example, all whitefish require good quality, well-oxygenated water in deep lakes. However they face a range of threats including various forms of pollution, sedimentation of spawning grounds and the introduction of coarse fish species such as Roach and Ruffe. The latter consume vulnerable whitefish eggs and fry and are implicated in the extinction of Vendace from Bassenthwaite Lake (Cumbria), and pose similar threats to the Welsh population of European Whitefish (the Gwyniad) in Lake Bala. As a conservation measure, Gwyniad eggs have been transferred to Llyn Arenig Fawr, a nearby cold water lake. The Scottish population of the European Whitefish (the Pollan) has also been successfully introduced as a conservation measure into two more sites: Loch Sloy and the Carron Valley Reservoir.

All stocking operations require the consent of the appropriate regulatory authority. This is a formal legal approval process to safeguard against some of the problems highlighted above. Before stock transfers are authorized, it may be necessary for the fish to be screened for parasites.

Further reading

Everard, M. (2006). *The Complete Book of the Roach*. Medlar Press, Ellesmere.

Everard, M. (2008). *The Little Book of Little Fishes*. Medlar Press, Ellesmere.

Everard, M. (2009). *Barbel River*. Medlar Press, Ellesmere.

Everard, M. (2011). *Dace: The Prince of the Stream*. Mpress, Romford.

Everard, M. (2012). *Fantastic Fishes: A Feast of Facts and Fables*. Ellesmere: Medlar Press.

Everard, M. and Knight, P. (2013). *Britain's Game Fishes: Celebration and Conservation of Salmonids*. Pelagic Press, Totnes.

Giles, N. (1993). *Freshwater Fish of the British Isles*. Swan Hill Press.

Greenhalgh, M. (2011). *Pocket Guide to Freshwater Fish of Britain and Europe*. Bounty Books.

Houghton, The Reverend W. (1879). *British Fresh-Water Fishes*. Reissued in a number of impressions, including Peerage Books, London (1984).

Maitland, P. S. (2004). *Keys to the Freshwater Fish of Britain and Ireland, with Notes on their Distribution and Ecology*. Freshwater Biological Association Scientific Publication No.62. The Freshwater Biological Association, Ambleside.

Maitland, P. S. and Linsell, K. (2006). *Guide to Freshwater Fish of Britain and Europe*. Philips.

Phillips, R., Rix, M. and Hurst, J. (1985). *Freshwater Fish of Britain, Ireland and Europe*. Pan Books.

Pinder, A. C. (2001). *Keys to Larval and Juvenile Stages of Coarse Fishes from Freshwaters in the British Isles*. Freshwater Biological Association Scientific Publication No.60. The Freshwater Biological Association, Ambleside.

Wheeler, A. (1969). *The Fishes of the British Isles and North West Europe*. Michigan State University Press.

Useful contacts

The Atlantic Salmon Trust
Suite 3/11, King James VI Business Centre, Friarton Road, Perth PH2 8DG, UK.
Tel.: +44 (0)1738 472032. Web: www.atlanticsalmontrust.org

The Freshwater Biological Association
The Ferry Landing, Far Sawrey, Ambleside, Cumbria LA22 0LP, UK.
Tel.: +44 (0)1539 442468. Web: www.fba.org.uk

Institute of Fisheries Management
PO Box 679, Hull HU5 9AX, UK.
Tel.: +44 (0)845 388 7012. Web: www.ifm.org.uk

Acknowledgements and photographic credits

In addition to my long-suffering family, Jackie and Daisy, many other people assisted me during the development of this book. Just a few of the more prominent people offering me support and/or encouragement were Scott West, Randy Velterop, Mike Ladle, Mike Elliott, Gary Newman, Steve Lockett and Adrian Pinder. Of course, I also relied upon a wide range of published and online sources. My particular thanks to the diligence of the **WILD**Guides team: Andy and Gill Swash, Robert Still and Steve Wright.

The production of this book would not have been possible without the contribution of the 23 photographers who kindly gave permission for their images to be reproduced. Grateful thanks are therefore extended to: Pete Adey, Jiri Bohdal (naturephoto-cz.com), Ricardo Roberto Fernández, Hans-Petter Fjeld, Rokus Groeneveld (diverosa.com), Derek Haslam, Hans Hillewaert, Lubomír Hlásek (hlasek.com), Dr Robert Holland, David Hosking/FLPA, Johnny Jensen (jjphoto.dk), Brian Morland, Jussi Murtosaari (Kuvaliiteri), Gary Newman, Jack Perks (jackperksphotography@hotmail.co.uk), Brian Rafferty, Peter Rolfe (www.crucians.org), J. C. Schou (Biopix.com), Jan Sevcik (naturephoto-cz.com), Niels Sloth (Biopix.com), Rudolf Svensen (uwphoto.no), Roger Tidman and Fernando Coello Vicente. Each of the images included in the book is listed below, with the photographer's name.

A number of people provided invaluable help in sourcing some of the images, and particular thanks are extended to Simon Pawley at the Freshwater Biological Association. Thanks are also due to Tony Andrews at The Atlantic Salmon Trust for kindly allowing Robin Ade's wonderful illustrations to be reproduced, and to Marjorie Hunter for facilitating so efficiently.

Cover Pike: M. Everard.
Frontispiece Three-spined Stickleback:
  Roger Tidman.
5 Dace: Jack Perks (jackperksphotography@
  hotmail.co.uk).
6 Sunglasses and pond net: M. Everard.
7 Signal Crayfish: M. Everard.
  New Zealand Pigmyweed: M. Everard.
  Kingfisher: Pete Adey.
8 Rainbow Trout: Jack Perks
  (jackperksphotography@hotmail.co.uk).
9 Orfe: N. Sloth (Biopix.com).
11 Atlantic Salmon life-cycle: Illustration
  by Robin Ade, reproduced courtesy
  of The Atlantic Salmon Trust (www.
  atlanticsalmontrust.org).
14 Bristol Avon: M. Everard.
15 River Otter, Devon: M. Everard.
16 River Wye, Powys: M. Everard.
17 Taw Estuary, North Devon: M. Everard.
18 Glacial lake, Llyn Cwellyn: M. Everard.
19 Lowland lake: M. Everard.
  Farmland pond: M. Everard.
20 Man-made reservoir: M. Everard.
21 Mature gravel pit: M. Everard.
  Canal: M. Everard.

22 Brown Trout: Lubomír Hlásek (hlasek.com).
  Dorsal fin: R. Tidman.
  Perch fin: Lubomír Hlásek (hlasek.com).
  Ruffe fin: Lubomír Hlásek (hlasek.com)
23 Mirror Carp scales: R. Tidman.
  Barbel scales: M. Everard.
  Sunbleak and Bleak lateral lines:
  Lubomír Hlásek (hlasek.com).
24 Dace: M. Everard
  Common Bream: M. Everard.
25 Bleak mouth: Lubomír Hlásek (hlasek.com).
  Dace mouth: Lubomír Hlásek (hlasek.com).
  Barbel mouth: M. Everard.
  Pike mouth: M. Everard.
26 Brown Trout: Pete Adey.
27 Rudd: Roger Tidman.
  Gudgeon: Roger Tidman.
  Common Bream: Jack Perks
  (jackperksphotography@hotmail.co.uk).
28 Grayling: Jack Perks
  (jackperksphotography@hotmail.co.uk).
29 Twaite Shad: Hans Hillewaert (licensed
  under the Creative Commons Attribution
  ShareAlike 3.0 License (creativecommons.
  org/licenses/by-sa/3.0/)).
31 Pike: Jack Perks (jackperksphotography@
  hotmail.co.uk).

Index

This index includes the English and *scientific*
names, and alternative names of all the fish
species covered in this book. **Bold names** are
the preferred English names used throughout
the book and **grey names** are alternative or local
names,

Bold numbers refer to the page on which the
main species account can be found.

Bold italicized blue numbers indicate the
location of other photographs or illustrations.

Normal black numbers refer to other key pages
where the species is mentioned.